To Caro...
Holid...
lo... ...chris
xxx

Dare
to Enter
His Presence

Suzanne Pillans

New Wine Press

New Wine Press
PO Box 17
Chichester
England PO20 6YB

ISBN: 1 903725 25 9

Other books available by the same author:

Search for Truth – a book of prose and poetry revealing God through
the beauty of nature.

The Biblical Approach to Basic Horsemanship – a book giving the basics
and attitudes to handling and riding horses, or handling any animal,
as the Bible shows us to.

Dare to Follow – a testimonial book showing what happens when we
follow God in obedience, as the Bible says we should; an exciting and
challenging book that could inspire you to go further with God and
lead you into an adventure of faith yourself. Published by New Wine
Press

Typeset by CRB Associates, Reepham, Norfolk.
Printed in England by Clays Ltd, St Ives plc.

Contents

Dedication

In dedication to God and His people, salvation being the greatest, most powerful and most meaningful gift in the universe. Prayer is the most glorious and heavenly contact that we can have with our creator God.

In pursuing the goal to know God more, He becomes our reality. He becomes more than simply believing in Him. He becomes our living faith.

He who was and is and is to come becomes our closest Father who never lets us down. He leads us in victory, answers our prayers and becomes everything we ever need. Full of love and compassion He leads us on through life and closer to Him.

The closer we live in His love the more we shall see Him move in our midst, from the simplest of things to the most miraculous, for He alone is our living God.

Acknowledgements

First I bow in grateful thanksgiving to Him who has entrusted me with the most awesome privilege to write on the most treasured subject of the universe, the worship of Him who created heaven and earth.

I can take no credit in writing this book, for I wrote it in prayer, as He opened the Scriptures to me and unveiled these priceless treasures that I have dared to write about.

I would also like to thank my father-in-law the Rev. Daile Pillans who, by his example, taught me what prayer was all about, and once prayed an hour for one person who came for communion, and preached as if to a full church. Twice I caught him come from his prayer study with his face shining from the Lord's presence. Also his son Wilfrid, to whom I have been married for almost 20 years, has given me very much support and backing in the Lord's work and has also typed this book. Rebecca, my 12-year-old daughter, understands and loves the Lord herself, and so willingly frees me to do the Lord's work.

I also thank God's people, especially the well known evangelists David Hathaway and Clive Corfield, who have also encouraged us much, not forgetting Rev. David Scott and Rev. Alan Stansbury who have pastored and encouraged us in God's work for over 20 years. Also my own parents, James and Joy Ratcliffe, who brought me up in the true values of life – thank you.

Preface

Suzanne was born in Bournemouth and grew up with horses. She became a Christian through the miraculous healing of her horse, Jacky Boy, and then dedicated her life to the Lord.

She is now married to Wilfrid. They have a daughter Rebecca. Suzanne and Wilfrid went to Bible College together. Suzanne was ordained as a minister in January 2003.

Suzanne's last book *Dare to Follow* spoke of their walk in obedience to the Lord, which led them into an exciting life of faith and ministry. This book is a teaching book on prayer and the glorious relationship that the Lord offers each one of us to have in Him, as we dare to enter into His presence.

Dare to Enter His Presence is also suitable to use as Bible studies, using one chapter per Bible study and then putting it into practice in prayer.

We have found that going straight into prayer has been far more effective than questions and answers, for in prayer the Lord intervenes and answers us Himself.

Foreword

I first met Suzanne and her family in February 2001 when they came to one of my meetings in England. She and her husband received healing, and she shared with me her urgent desire to come to our 'Fire Over Jerusalem' Convention in May later that same year.

Suzanne is a wife and mother, a hard-working owner of a successful horse-riding school, a quiet but determined person with a great hunger and thirst for God. At the time when I first met her, her key scripture for two years had been John 7:38: *'He who believes in me, as the scripture has said, "Out of his heart shall flow rivers of living water."'* For two years she had cried out, 'But there's no water flowing through my life!' She read every book on revival, every book on prayer. She came to our 'Fire Over Jerusalem' Convention in Israel in May 2001 – and the fire fell – on her!

Suzanne told me that, whilst in prayer with guests at the Convention from Africa, the Lord said to her, 'Abide in Me and I shall surely abide in you wherever I send you.' She went on to say, 'These words changed my life, and from that time the Lord began to heal people as I laid hands on them.' Suzanne had the courage and faith to obey God – and He began a new ministry through her.

This book is the evidence of the power and anointing which has begun to follow her ministry, firstly in the 'Fire over Kenya' Conference, then wherever she has gone, especially in Africa, but also in her own home surroundings, in obedience to the call of God. Suzanne has a very practical experience with the Lord which relates to everyday experience. She shows in this book that God uses the ordinary people to demonstrate His power and glory. When God called an 80-year-old man called Moses to become the one who would lead the Jewish people out of captivity in Egypt, Moses was just a shepherd with a family to support. The Bible says that not many high or mighty are called, but *'God has chosen the weak to confound the mighty.'*

The ministry and the healings continue, as Suzanne continues to believe God. The challenge is this; Jesus said: *'He who believes in me ... "Out of his heart shall flow rivers of living water."'* Talk is not enough – we need this demonstration of the power of Jesus in the world today! Through Suzanne – but also through **you**!

David Hathaway
Evangelist
President of Eurovision

Chapter 1

To Know Him – Who He Is

The more we know God, the greater our joy. The more we know the Scriptures, the more we may know Him, know Him while He may still be found, while we are alive. Search for Him in the Bible, search for Him in prayer and He will meet you right there. He will reveal to you His great truths, His glorious presence, His exceeding joy. Like Moses, He may even allow you a glimpse of His glory, His majesty, His everlasting light.

Right from the beginning of time God has wanted man to know Him; to know Him as their only true God, but to also know Him like Moses did, in close fellowship with Himself, for man is created to have fellowship with God.

God has not only spoken to man but has also demonstrated His power and majesty, love and concern, mercy and compassion. He has truly demonstrated to man that He alone is God, there is no other. These demonstrations He has carried out through the centuries right to this very day for He is the same God, yesterday, today and forever.

Let us start in Exodus 7:5:

> *'And the Egyptians shall know that I am the LORD, when I stretch forth my hand upon Egypt and bring out the people of Israel from among them.'*

He first said what He was going to do before He did it. Then in Exodus 18:11:

> *'Now I know that the* LORD *is greater than all gods, because he delivered the people from under the hand of the Egyptians, when they dealt arrogantly with them.'*

The Lord then tells the world why He did this in Exodus 29:46:

> *'And they shall know that I am the* LORD *their God, who brought them forth out of the land of Egypt that I might dwell among them; I am the* LORD *their God.'*

God does not leave it here. He wants to tell all generations, as the next three scriptures show:

> *'Say to the people of Israel, "You shall keep my sabbaths, for this is a sign between me and you throughout your generations, that you may know that I, the* LORD, *sanctify you."'*
>
> (Exodus 31:13)

> *'that your generations may know that I made the people of Israel dwell in booths when I brought them out of the land of Egypt; I am the* LORD *your God.'*   (Leviticus 23:43)

> *'To you it was shown, that you might know that the* LORD *is God; there is no other besides him. Out of heaven he let you hear his voice, that he might discipline you; and on earth he let you see his great fire, and you heard his words out of the midst of the fire. And because he loved your fathers and chose their descendants after them, and brought you out of Egypt with his own presence, by his great power, driving out before you nations greater and mightier than yourselves, to bring you in, to give you their land for an inheritance, as at this*

day; know therefore this day, and lay it to your heart, that the
LORD is God in heaven above and on the earth beneath; there
is no other.'   (Deuteronomy 4:35–39)

Right through history God has spoken through His
prophets; God has demonstrated His power. He has set the
captives free, He has healed the sick, He has showed His love
and compassion for us. Then Jesus came and fulfilled the Old
Testament with His own life, even dying on the cross:

'For God so loved the world that he gave his only Son, that
whoever believes in him should not perish but have eternal
life.'   (John 3:16)

The life of Jesus changed history as millions realised their
need for God, turning from the new Greek philosophy that
man is God to their new found faith and truth in Jesus. As
the news of Jesus spread throughout the known world of
Greece and Rome, it forced the ideal of that day under-
ground, not to rear its ugly head again until our modern
times as humanism.

Here in our modern times God is still at work, speaking to
His people and demonstrating His power. He can use anyone
to speak through or demonstrate His power. He does not
only use the great evangelists but normal people like you
and me.

I saw His power at work in a little village of Migowi
in Malawi. There was one believer, a pastor called Duncan,
who built a mud brick church with a grass roof and began
to preach Jesus to the community. They would come to
his church, but refused to believe in miracles or healing.
Duncan had got hold of a magazine from an organisation
called Eurovision run by the well known evangelist David
Hathaway. Duncan was so desperate with the unbelief of the

people that he wrote to Eurovision to send someone to them.

Through this request I was offered the chance to go to Malawi. As I already had contacts in South Africa and Kenya, it was quiet easy to put together a fairly busy itinerary.

First the Lord gave me a vision of many people in brightly-coloured clothing coming down rocky hills to an outdoor crusade. I was speaking with a new authority and boldness that almost shocked me in the vision and the people were responding. The vision ended here.

Then the Lord also spoke to me. This is what I believe He said: 'Tell My people I love them, tell My people to wake up, for the drought in their hearts is over and past and the sound of rain approaches and I am prepared to answer My people even as they ask, and as they wait upon Me, so I shall come down upon them.'

I knew God was calling me to go, even alone, so within two weeks everything was organised and I flew to South Africa.

Right from the first talk I saw the prophecy the Lord had given me come true in South Africa, Kenya and Malawi, but Malawi was definitely the most exciting.

I arrived to a desperate situation of severe drought, searing heat, sickness and unbelief. Three people had already died of starvation. They were living on leaves cooked in ashes to soften them, and cut stalks. I called out to God. Only He could help.

We had arrived on the Monday evening and I was shown to my room in a mud hut and given a grass mat to sleep on, on the floor. I blew up my lilo, placed it on the mat and crawled into my sleeping bag. Half an hour later I opened my eyes, aware of a noise beside me. I put on my torch and it shone into the eyes of a huge rat about a foot from my face. I accidentally let out a scream. 'L-o-r-d!' I called out. I had been prepared for sleeping on the floor, but not for the wildlife! What do I do now? Ah! The mosquito net. Soon I had it tied to the roof and climbed into my little secluded tent and slept well. Now the rats could not climb over me. Then I thought what a privilege this was, to taste how Jesus had to live in similar conditions two thousand years ago. Tomorrow was to be my day off to settle in. I wondered how the Lord might get the people to come this week. The Lord always has a plan.

The light of dawn was very welcome, so I got up early. When I went outside at 6.30 a.m. I found four people waiting for me. They were in too much pain to walk any further to the market to sell their wares in order to buy some food. They had heard that I was coming, so why not give it a try? Two had very bad arthritis, one had very sore feet and the other one, Aliane, was suffering with chest and stomach problems caused by HIV AIDS. I prayed for them one by one and every trace of pain and symptoms left. Jesus had healed all four of them there and then. They then ran to the market.

By 9.30 a.m. people began to come, as the four ladies were telling everyone that Jesus had healed them. By 2.00 p.m. the church was full to capacity with over 150 people inside and outside the church. I gave the gospel message. Sixty-one became Christians and the Lord healed a further eight people. We then went to the rugby field and walked around it seven times to break the strongholds of unbelief and other things in the community.

By 6.30 on Wednesday morning people were already arriving to receive their healings. A further 28 were healed by Jesus and 78 more people became Christians, including the chief. They could not wait for the crusade to start. I said to Duncan, 'Forget hiring the generator. Here, buy some food for yourself and all these people.' There was much rejoicing at the healings and more rejoicing at the food.

At 2.00 p.m. the crusade began at the rugby field. Many people came, more and more, just as I had seen in the vision.

This caused me to speak more boldly than ever before. I spoke on believing God. 'Has anyone ever thought of praying for rain?' I asked. No one had. I then asked if anyone would like to become a Christian and about 400 rushed forward. I led them through the sinner's prayer and told them how to live their new found faith in Jesus. We then started to pray again. The pastor came up to me and said, 'They are now praying for rain.' They then went and sat down.

I said, 'The sick may now come forward.' About 300 rushed forward. I thought, 'Lord, how do I pray for all these people?' I told them that Jesus was going to heal them right where they were and said, 'Put your own hand on the sick area or pain.' I said the prayer and some of them got very excited. Jesus had healed them and over 40 rushed forward wanting to testify about their healings.

The people were now leaping with excitement, laughing, crying with joy, hollering, jumping up and down. 'Jesus is passing by us!' they shouted. Now the very sick were coming forward to be prayed for one by one. Jesus was healing all of them and they immediately testified over the mike. The crowd became even more excited and almost crushed me in their urgency to get healed. The next man in front of me was almost standing on my feet and a bit too close for me to even move. He was a leper on crutches. I stopped a moment to ask God, 'How do I pray for him?' I looked up, as it appeared to be getting rather dark and a wind was blowing. I saw black clouds blowing over us and right there and then it began to rain. The meeting had to stop. Now the people were even more excited, for God had answered their prayer within the hour! I told the sick to come back tomorrow and the whole crusade ran home in the rain praising God.

Benedicto, the leper, was there first the next morning. Only the sick came, as everyone else was now planting seeds. I prayed for Benedicto and the Lord removed every trace of pain, so that he walked without crutches. He believed he was healed. A further 27 people were healed and another 12 became Christians.

The next day, Friday, we had a word from the chief. He said, 'Never have I seen anything like Wednesday's crusade, the demonstration of the power of Jesus, Jesus healing the sick and sending rain when the people prayed for it. I am very very happy and so is the whole community.'

By this time I was learning to pray for the people in sections as a result of my time with the Lord that morning. I felt Him say to me, 'Stop fretting, My child. Relax and flow with Me, for I am in control. I shall not let you get crushed by the people. Have I not called you here? Will I not protect you? Will I not guide you in what to say? Simply relax and yield to My hands and we shall flow together, for I love to bless my people, I love to heal the sick. I love to set them free. I came to give life and life in abundance, so rest in Me, My child, and simply let Me do it.'

What encouragement that was, and it was then that I received the idea to pray for them in groups. I asked for all those with head problems to come forward; a group of 14 came forward and 14 were healed. Then I prayed for further groups: one of 15 with stomach problems, one of 10 with arthritis, one of 5 with sore feet, another of 4 who were blind, and so on. Eventually a further 75 people received their healing. I then spoke more on the Holy Spirit and every person came forward to get baptised in the Holy Spirit. It was a wonderful day.

By Saturday almost the entire community had become Christians. Another 5 became Christians and a further 6 received healing.

To see the Lord answer prayer like this is awesome – seeing God bigger than ever before, not just loving but also holy, awesome and life-changing. I felt as though I was only beginning to discover God here with these people, our God who answers prayers even as we ask, our Jesus who is alive right now amongst us.

The Lord was not finished either. I had left only enough food to last until just after Christmas and the cheque I had given Duncan for more food could not be cashed. On Saturday at 4.00 a.m. I interceded for these people and repented for not leaving Duncan with more money for food. There was no way to get money to Duncan now.

It appeared that the Lord was asking me to phone a certain person. I obeyed and phoned telling the man of this problem.

'A friend of ours from our church has just moved to Blantyre,' he said. ' I will phone him now and see if he can help.'

By 10.00 a.m. it was all organised. All we had to do was put the money in his account here in Oxford, and he was prepared to help us get food to them until their harvest. By Tuesday he had delivered 24 sacks of maize to the doorstep of a very surprised Duncan. Then our church said they would help with £500 per month until harvest. Then another church gave a £1,000 for food. I never asked for a penny but our God cares, not only for the church members, but for the whole community. What a mighty God we serve. By sending rain within the hour of the people's prayer, He had demonstrated to them that He alone is God. That was enough for the entire community to become Christians. Then to be provided with food right up to a good harvest showed them just how much God loved them. He had shown them salvation, healed the sick, answered their prayer for rain, sent them food until their harvest, and blessed them with a good harvest.

Other villages also heard what happened in Migowi which caused further invitations and many more people to become Christians and receive their healings in the following visit.

They have now bought some land and are building a church.

Chapter 2

To Know Him by Experience

The amount that we grow to know our God will determine our bottom line and the degree that we will be able to walk our life of faith.

Let us start by David's word to Solomon in 1 Chronicles 28:9:

> 'And you, Solomon my son, know the God of your father, and serve him with a whole heart and with a willing mind; for the LORD searches all hearts, and understands every plan and thought. If you seek him, he will be found by you; but if you forsake him, he will cast you off for ever.'

Let us now look at a couple of key verses: the first a 'bottom line' for Job, the second a 'bottom line' for David.

> 'For I know that my Redeemer lives, and at last he will stand upon the earth.'   (Job 19:25)

This was Job's 'bottom line' that enabled him to endure his suffering victoriously, and brought God's blessing upon his life to restore to him double what he had before.

Now we will look at David's life and discover his 'bottom line'. First his prayer found in Psalm 25:4–5:

> *'Make me to know thy ways, O LORD;*
>   *teach me thy paths.*
> *Lead me in thy truth, and teach me,*
>   *for thou art the God of my salvation;*
>   *for thee I wait all the day long.'*

David began his walk with God as a humble shepherd boy. It was his longing to know God that made him brave, that turned him into a great leader. He knew who God was, he spent much time with God, and God met him there and answered his prayer. He taught David His ways. That is why David saw God as greater than Goliath. He knew that with God on his side, he could conquer Goliath.

> *'Then David said to the Philistine, "You come to me with a sword and with a spear and with a javelin; but I come to you in the name of the LORD of hosts, the God of the armies of Israel, whom you have defied. This day the LORD will deliver you into my hand, and I will strike you down, and cut off your head; and I will give the dead bodies of the host of the Philistines this day to the birds of the air and to the wild beasts of the earth; that all the earth may know that there is a God in Israel, and that all this assembly may know that the LORD saves not with sword and spear; for the battle is the LORD's and he will give you into our hand." When the Philistine arose and came and drew near to meet David, David ran quickly toward the battle line to meet the Philistine. And David put his hand in his bag and took out a stone, and slung it, and struck the Philistine on his forehead; the stone sank into the forehead, and he fell on his face to the ground.'*   (1 Samuel 17:45–49)

David's bottom line was Psalm 56:9:

> *'Then my enemies will be turned back*
> *in the day when I call.*
> *This I know, that God is for me.'*

Where is our bottom line? My own thoughts go back to a time I had gone out to Kenya to support a man of God with a powerful healing ministry. Only one problem: near to the last moment he emailed us to say he could no longer come as a speaker!

It was now too late to cancel the 'Fire Over Kenya' Conference. There was only one thing to do, I had to step into his shoes as speaker and pray for the sick.

Once in Kenya I did not feel quiet so brave. Bala was two hours off any road. We had to drive over rough terrain, hills, and grasslands, past mud rondavals and two funerals taking place on the way. I was told six people were dying of AIDS or disease every day.

We arrived at dusk at the Bishop's mud house and he gave us a lantern and showed us where Ruth and I were to sleep.

Early next morning Ruth and I went to find a place outside to pray. We sat down on a couple of rocks feeling totally inadequate, hopeless and way out of our depth. In fact we wondered what we were doing, even coming to such a place. Only God could do something. One thing was certain, we could do nothing. We cried out to God like never before. We literally cried out for the desperate needs of the people.

After a good half hour of desperate crying, a quiet came over us and I believe I heard God speak: 'If I can cry through your eyes like this, I can also heal through your hands like this.' This was the beginning of a healing ministry.

We walked back to the kraal. There was a woman there with her son falling all over the room. He could not stand even for a second before he fell in another direction. 'Deliver my son from these demons,' she shouted.

I stared, wanting to run from this but fought to stand my ground.

'Please deliver my son from these demons,' she shouted again.

'Lord, help me I whispered,' and pointing at the falling boy, shouted, 'Demons, come out in the name of **Jesus**.'

The boy stood up, still crying but normal, still a bit confused, but totally set free.

'Thank you,' said his mom. 'I knew you could help.'

'**Jesus** did it,' I replied.

'I know He did,' she said. 'Goodbye.' And she and her son calmly walked home.

The crusade started that evening. I gave a simple gospel message and then asked the sick to come forward. Thirty people rushed forward.

To my horror the first three were blind. 'Lord,' I prayed, 'Help!' I then remembered that this was similar to Reinhard Bonnke's first attempt to pray for the sick. 'Lord, can I use the same words as Reinhard Bonnke?' I asked.

It seemed alright, so I went up to the first one and in a German accent said, 'Blind eyes, open in the name of **Jesus**.'

'I can see,' the lady shouted.

'What?'

'I can see,' she repeated.

'Can you really see properly?' I ask again.

'Yes, I can really see.'

'Go and testify on the mike,' I told her.

I then went to the second person and the same thing happened. She could suddenly see. Then the third person also could instantly see.

The fourth person had malaria, so I cast the malaria out in Jesus' name and within one minute her temperature was down to normal. She was healed. The next person had fallen down a cliff onto his head causing his left arm to go limp. I prayed over his head and suddenly his arm came alive. He could move it, he was healed.

All thirty people were healed by Jesus that night and by the end of the conference two hundred and fifty people had received their healings from Jesus.

After the crusade Ruth had to go home. Bishop Dominic, the driver, the interpreter and I visited different churches for the remaining week. One problem was that the witch-doctors were very angry about the healings as they were losing income as a result. They were now after me and knew the route we were travelling. For two nights now they had been drumming and doing frenzy dancing and chanting curses outside my very hotel window!

'Lord,' I cried, 'please protect me from these witch-doctors.'

'Rest in Me,' I felt the Lord say, 'for I am in complete control. I know the bondage My people here are under, but the bondage of disease and death shall be lifted, for I shall lift it. Walk forth in Me, My child, for no evil shall touch you. Rest in Me, My child, for it is I that shall do it through you. Yes, walk in oneness with Me, your hand placed in mine and this work we shall do together.'

This word from the Lord strengthened me so much that I was able to come against their curses to break up or confuse the three meetings that day. The Lord strengthened me so much that I did not even care if there was an army of witch-doctors, for I suddenly saw God as so much greater. I went to the meetings to see a wonderful move of God as a further forty seven people received their healings and almost every-one received the baptism of the Holy Spirit.

Suddenly I saw the truth of Psalm 56:9:

> *'Then my enemies will be turned back*
> *in the day when I call.*
> *This I know, that God is for me.'*

I had no further problems from the witch-doctors, and the following year most of the witch-doctors' families had become Christians. Margaret, a wife of a well known witch-doctor, had been a Christian for four months. She had been blind for four years as a result of a snake bite. I prayed for her and the Lord completely restored her eyesight within about two minutes. What a wonderful God we serve. My bottom line was realised: 'My God is great, my God can do anything He wants to do.'

To find our bottom line is to know God, to know Him by our own experience of Him. To get to know God is to simply spend time in His presence. There is no other way. We either get to know Him by spending time with Him or we never get to know Him. The more time we spend in His presence, the more we will get to know Him. There are many different dimensions of knowing Him, but in each Jesus is with you at your side leading you on. Jeremiah 24:7 says:

> *'I will give them a heart to know that I am the LORD; and they shall be my people and I will be their God, for they shall return to me with their whole heart.'*

First we need to seek Him with our whole hearts.

Paul prayed in Ephesians 1:17–19:

> *'that the God of our Lord Jesus Christ, the Father of glory, may give you a spirit of wisdom and of revelation in the knowledge of him, having the eyes of your hearts enlightened, that you may know what is the hope to which he has called you, what are the riches of his glorious inheritance in the saints, and what is the immeasurable greatness of his power in us who believe, according to the working of his great might.'*

As we begin to seek Him, He will also reveal to us His revelations in greater detail.

Let's look at John 17:2–3:

> *'since thou hast given him power over all flesh, to give eternal life to all whom thou hast given him. And this is eternal life, that they know thee the only true God, and Jesus Christ whom thou hast sent.'*

Then read from John 17:6–8:

> *'I have manifested thy name to the men whom thou gavest me out of the world; thine thy were, and thou gavest them to me, and they have kept thy word. Now they know that everything that thou hast given me is from thee; for I have given them the words which thou gavest me, and they have received them and know in truth that I came from thee; and they have believed that thou didst send me.'*

This passage shows us how much God loves us. He shows us that we can have certainty and know in truth that Jesus came from the Father and He gives us security in Him and identity with Him as we come to know Him more and more. This is confirmed even more in John 10:14:

> *'I am the good shepherd; I know my own and my own know me.'*

When we know we belong to God then John 17:3 also becomes our destiny. This certainty, security and identity that we know God knows us and we know Him then becomes even deeper as John 17:23 reveals:

> *'I in them and thou in me, that they may become perfectly one, so that the world may know that thou hast sent me and hast loved them even as thou hast loved me.'*

Do you know that God loves you so much? Is your heart searching for Him? Then receive His love, for He loves you and wants you to respond to Him, to come to know Him more.

Do not allow any unworthiness or fear of rejection stop you from knowing Him as I once did. Do not make the same mistake as I did and many do, who listen to the lies of Satan and feel unworthy, rather than the truth of God.

I felt like that until one day I was at a conference in Toronto. I had a vision of the Lord putting His hand within me, taking out my heart, cupping it in His hand tenderly as He looked at it. Then suddenly He closed His other hand over it and walked off with it, ending the vision.

I sat up startled. 'He's walked off with my heart. He did not put it back!' Then it dawned on me, 'He has my heart! That means I truly belong to Him.'

'You can have my heart, Lord Jesus,' I called out loud, 'I never want it back.'

Hopefully He does not have to go that far for all of us. The moment we give Jesus our heart, we should know that He has received it, for He knows our hearts, He knows the hearts that reach out to Him.

Jeremiah 12:3 says:

> 'But thou, O LORD, knowest me,
>   thou seest me, and triest my mind towards thee.

Acts 15:8 says:

> 'And God who knows the heart bore witness to them, giving
> them the Holy Spirit just as he did to us.'

Once we receive the Holy Spirit within our hearts we know beyond all measure that He knows us and He has come to live within us. Suddenly John 17:23 comes alive, *'I in them and thou in me.'*

If you have not already received the Holy Spirit and would like to, for the Holy Spirit will help lead you into the Holy presence of God, then just pray this simple prayer:

> Dear Lord, I come to You as I am. Please forgive me where I have sinned against You in thought, in word, in deed and in things I have left undone. Please forgive me and come into my heart and baptise me in the Holy Spirit. Thank You, Lord. Amen.

Now just simply receive Him, and open your heart to Him. You may even feel a warm glow within, but even if you feel nothing know that your prayer is answered. You are now baptised in the Holy Spirit. The Bible will be easier to read, for you will begin to understand it more and as you worship God. You will know a deeper and fuller relationship with Him. You will know with all certainty that you belong to Him and that He loves you so very much.

You will also discover that you should not just read the Bible, but live it, for the Bible is the living Word of God and behind every sentence is the power of heaven. It's as we walk the Scriptures in faith that the Lord can answer. There has to be a need for a miracle or healing to occur. Only as we live the Word will the Word become active and effective in our lives.

Chapter 3

Abide in Him

It was at the garden tomb in Jerusalem while receiving Holy Communion that I felt the Lord say these words to me: 'Take part in Me and in all where I will lead you, and you surely shall take part in Me. Abide in Me and I shall surely abide in you.' These words struck me so deeply they caused tears.

The Lord later led me to John 15:7–11:

> 'If you abide in me, and my words abide in you, ask whatever you will, and it shall be done for you. By this my Father is glorified, that you bear much fruit, and so prove to be my disciples. As the Father has loved me, so I have loved you; abide in my love. If you keep my commandments, you will abide in my love, just as I have kept my Father's commandments and abide in His love. These things I have spoken to you, that my joy may be in you, and that your joy may be full.'

These verses say so much. What really stood out for me, though, was to abide in His love. If we abide in His love it will become natural for His words to abide in us, for us to keep His commandments and by doing this, we will also experience His joy.

This was then confirmed in 1 Corinthians 13:13:

> *'So faith, hope, love abide, these three; but the greatest of these is love.'*

So this means one needs to allow God to love us and we need to abide in His love. The Lord was to teach me this over the next year. It is also important to listen when the Lord speaks to you, for His words will encourage you so much. I always keep a prayer diary where I write down everything that I believe the Lord is trying to say to me. To make sure that I hear from the Lord and no other voice I will make sure I have the armour of the Holy Spirit on as in Ephesians 6:14–18 and plead the blood of Jesus as protection as they did in Hebrews 10:18–25, for the devil cannot stand the blood of Jesus and will run from it. I believe I am then ready for anything the Lord may want to do or say to me. I will share a couple of the words on love that I believe the Lord gave to me, which transformed me so much.

About three months after the word at the garden tomb, I believe the Lord said these words:

> 'Yes, My child, abide in My love and My love shall abide in you. Wherever you are, receive this love, My child, for you are mine. Live in My love and you shall also walk in My love. Allow My Holy Spirit to infuse you with My love that you may learn to walk in love. Let My Holy Spirit infuse your mind for it still thinks in worldly ways and you still walk in worldly ways.
>
> Yes, My child, you need to spend much time in My presence, that you may learn My ways, think with My mind and walk in My ways. Only in fellowship with Myself can My love break down your outward hard crust and break forth from you in a new love and compassion

that I have for My children, My love that can set free, deliver, heal and make whole.'

This word enabled me to search my heart and discover the worldly ways I was still thinking and walking in. I then repented of these worldly ways as 1 John 3:6 says:

'No one who abides in him sins; no one who sins has either seen him or known him.'

I then came to the Lord daily simply to spend time in His presence, to come to know Him more and to drink of His love and beauty.

A month later, I believe the Lord spoke to me again as I was spending time waiting on Him:

'Yes, My child, the more you drink of My love, the more you abide in My love. You drink and you live in Me and so shall your life be filled with My love, and this has to overflow. It has to overflow into rivers of living water, the water of love that has My power to heal, that has My power to deliver, that has My power to enable people to become whole. Yes, My child, it's My love that has My power, for it is My love which is the living waters of life.'

This word came to me as a wonderful revelation and a new understanding. I turned to John 7:37–38 and read with new understanding:

'On the last day of the feast, the great day, Jesus stood up and proclaimed, "If any one thirst, let him come to me and drink. He who believes in me, as the scripture has said, 'Out of his heart shall flow rivers of living water.'"'

'Is love the main substance of the Holy Spirit then?' I

questioned. It appeared to me that it was, for if we are filled with God's love we will then serve Him out of love and not through duty or any other motive.

It appeared that to abide in Him is to abide in His love, as the Lord seemed to confirm to me the following month, after I had seen the Lord heal others when I prayed for them. He also called me His daughter for the first time rather than His child. I felt I had become closer to Him.

This is what I believe He said:

> 'My daughter, it is because you abide in Me that I also abide in you. When I abide in you miracles will happen and greater than these will happen when you abide in My love, for then I can live in union with you, for then I can reach out to those in real need through you. Abide in Me, my daughter, and I shall surely abide in you.'

Psalm 91:1–2 says:

> *'He who dwells in the shelter of the Most High,*
> *who abides in the shadow of the Almighty,*
> *will say to the LORD, "My refuge and my fortress;*
> *my God, in whom I trust."'*

By abiding in the Lord, in His shelter, in His shadow of love and protection, He prepares us in love to reach out to others as in 1 John 4:11–12:

> *'Beloved, if God so loved us, we also ought to love one another. No man has ever seen God; if we love one another, God abides in us and His love is perfected in us.'*

This love can become more and more perfected in us over time. This love does not only cause us to love one another, but also prepares us for eternal life as John says in 1 John 2:24–25:

> *'Let what you heard from the beginning abide in you. If what you heard from the beginning abides in you, then you will abide in the Son and in the Father. And this is what he has promised us, eternal life.'*

Abiding in Him, abiding in His love, is though only the preparation for even more, a growing in Him, a growing in love, a walking in love.

On the plane on my first visit to Kenya I learnt from a book by Rees Howells that there are degrees, or stages, in abiding. The deeper the oneness, the more the power of the risen life of Christ can operate through the channel and new positions of spiritual authority can be gained. We need to abide without being called to abide. We need to walk in that position.

Further to that, from a channel you can become a branch, a branch where His sap can pour through you that produces much fruit.

I then felt the Lord say, 'Sit up. I want to speak to you.'

I did and I asked Him, 'Lord, am I a channel or a branch?'

He said, 'A channel is used now and then, a branch is used all the time. A channel is as a watering can, the branch is there continually. As you abide in Me continually, you shall become as a branch. *Abide in Me and I shall surely abide in you* was My command. Abide in Me now and I shall abide in you now. You hear Me speak to you. That is because you abide in Me, but a deeper level awaits. As you abide in Me so shall you become more open to My presence, My guiding touch, My silent voice. This demands a closer walk, a keener ear and sensitivity.'

'Lord, how?' I asked.

'That's right by receiving, receiving My presence more and more. Yes, allow Me to envelope your life. If you want to

move in the supernatural, you must also receive of it, from
Me, by My Holy Spirit. If you want to be a branch you need
to graft yourself to Me and so shall My Holy Spirit flow
through you to My people. Then there will be greater results
as you pray for them. As you are learning to hear and to
listen you shall speak forth My word with power. It's a total
reliance on Me that I call you to. As you hear and obey I will
do the rest.'

I thanked the Lord for His wonderful word to me and
reached out for my Bible.

John 15:4–11:

> 'Abide in me, and I in you. As the branch cannot bear fruit by
> itself, unless it abides in the vine, neither can you, unless you
> abide in me. I am the vine, you are the branches. He who
> abides in me, and I in him, he it is that bears much fruit, for
> apart from me you can do nothing. If a man does not abide in
> me, he is cast forth as a branch and withers; and the
> branches are gathered, thrown into the fire and burned. If
> you abide in me, and my words abide in you, ask whatever
> you will, and it shall be done for you. By this my Father is
> glorified, that you bear much fruit, and so prove to be my
> disciples. As the Father has loved me, so have I loved you;
> abide in my love. If you keep my commandments, you will
> abide in my love, just as I have kept my Father's command-
> ments and abide in his love. These things I have spoken to
> you, that my joy may be in you, and that your joy may be
> full.'

It is not enough to just know what the Word says. We have
to live it, then we will see results. Little did I know then, that
in the following week I would see the Lord heal 250 people
in front of me. I saw the Lord's glorious love and compassion
for His people and almost stood back from it myself. Only
during the following year was the Lord able to pour a drop

of that love and compassion for others into my own heart, but I still had a lot to learn. I still had to learn how to enter His presence more and after that, to learn how to dwell in His glorious presence, so very much more of His glorious truths to learn and love.

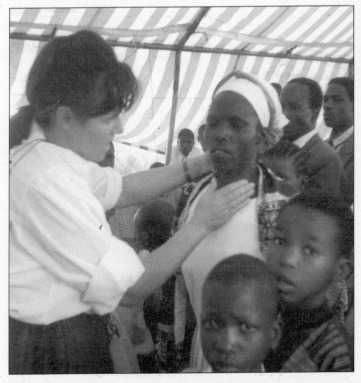

Suzanne praying for healing at the Fire Over Kenya conference where she saw 250 people healed in one week

Chapter 4

Enter into His Presence

Wherever I go to speak, people come up and ask, 'How do we come into the presence of God?' This is the reason I am writing this book; to share with others from a biblical perspective, as well as by experience, how I myself learnt to enter His glorious presence.

The Lord has shown us how to enter His presence by the way He showed Moses in the building of the tabernacle, where every detail has meaning. That would take a book and there are excellent books on the subject, so we will only mention the meaning of the three areas that connect with the different levels of prayer and how to enter the presence of God.

The first area is the outer court. This was used in the Old Testament for sacrificing animals for the forgiveness of sin. In the New Testament Jesus fulfilled the forgiveness of sin by His own sacrifice of dying on the cross and rising on the third day that those of us who believe in Him shall not die but have everlasting life, as 1 Peter 2:24 says:

'He himself bore our sins in his body on the tree, that we might die to sin and live to righteousness. By his wounds you have been healed.'

Hebrews 9:12–14 says:

> *'He entered once for all into the Holy Place, taking not the blood of goats and calves but his own blood, thus securing an eternal redemption. For if the sprinkling of defiled persons with the blood of goats and bulls and with the ashes of a heifer sanctifies for the purification of the flesh, how much more shall the blood of Christ, who through the eternal Spirit offered himself without blemish to God, purify your conscience from dead works to serve the living God.'*

So the only way into the presence of God is through the cross, the outer court first that any sin in us can be dealt with. After we have confessed any sin we can now enter into the next area as in Psalm 100:4:

> *'Enter his gates with thanksgiving,*
> *   and his courts with praise!*
> *   Give thanks to him, bless his name.'*

We now leave the outer area behind, where we asked God to forgive us, bless us, help us, to come into the next area where we thank Him, praise Him, bless Him. This is a deeper area; here we can also pray for others. There is only one problem. This is where many people stop. They do not seem to realise there is yet another area, a deeper level of coming right into the very presence of God. This third area is called the Holy of Holies. In the Old Testament the priest was only allowed in there once a year. It was the place where the Ark of the Covenant was kept covered by two cherubim with wings covering the presence of God.

The moment Jesus died on the cross the curtain was torn from top to bottom, meaning all of us are now invited into the Holy of Holies, the very presence of God as in Hebrews 10:19–22:

'Therefore, brethren, since we have confidence to enter the sanctuary by the blood of Jesus, by the new and living way which he opened for us through the curtain, that is, through his flesh, and since we have a great high priest over the house of God, let us draw near with a true heart in full assurance of faith, with our hearts sprinkled clean from an evil conscience and our bodies washed with pure water.'

People may ask, 'What is this entering the presence of God? Are we not always in the presence of God?' Yes, God is with the believer all the time. Yes, we are in His presence all the time. But there is a deeper level. It is the conscious presence of the Lord we seek, the conscious presence that one is able to experience and enjoy. This is possible and this is real.

One can be married and know you are loved, but it is not enough to just know it. You also want to experience that love, to feel that love. It is exactly the same with the Lord.

To experience the conscious presence of love, joy and peace that the Lord fills us with, you have to put in effort to know Him, just as you would a person. To direct your thoughts, attention and love on Him, simply your full focus that is all, and He will meet you there.

You will experience His touch on your heart, and I am sure everyone wants to experience this. We do not need to settle for less. For me, I choose to get as close to the Lord as humanly possible and that is to enter right into His glorious presence, and then stay there – right in the heavenly conscious presence of our living God. Here you can actually feel His touch upon your life.

The next stage is to enter in, concentrate fully on the Lord, adore Him, worship Him, tell Him how much you love Him., carry on, press in, until He meets you there. For worship always goes ahead of you entering in, just as the incense from the altar of incense entered the Holy of Holies as a form of worship and adoration before the priest could enter into this holy area.

Sometimes it's not easy. It is as if He is testing you to see how determined you are, how desperate, how much you long to come into His presence. This could take minutes, this could take hours. At first it could take me up to seven hours to enter His presence. Once it took all night and up to 11.00 a.m. the following morning, just five minutes before I was due to speak. But then I felt His presence and I was able to speak under His anointing. The more you do it, the easier it becomes. Once you enter in you will know it, you will feel His presence surround you, you will be filled with His love, His joy, His peace.

So you enter into His presence in worship. Once in His presence you may just rest in Him. Just rest and enjoy His beautiful presence. It is here that the Lord may wish to speak to you, or teach you, or open the Scriptures to you. It is here I always have a pen and note book ready, for you are quiet and able to write surrounded by His presence. In fact some of us can only write when within the presence of God, for it is He who gives us what to write.

Sometimes the Holy Spirit will direct you to intercede for someone. Always obey this prompting, for the Lord is waiting to answer this prayer. He is always looking for intercessors to prompt, to intercede for various people or situations, as He has chosen to work through man. Therefore He has chosen to move, as we pray. This type of prayer is often urgent and very effective, as the Lord answers almost the moment we pray.

When we realise the importance of prayer as well as the joy of His glorious presence we will look forward to our time with Him. We will want to come into His presence every day of our lives. We will also want to spend more time with the Lord. We will come to know Him at deeper and deeper levels until we simply do not ever wish to come out of His beautiful presence.

Is this possible? Yes it is, for the Bible now leads us deeper in prayer. The Bible tells us to dwell in His presence continually. Just as the lamp stand was lit in the tabernacle twenty-four hours a day, seven days a week, the revelation of God is to be received twenty four hours a day. We should never stop receiving from Jesus or from the Word of God. Then our hearts will be lit by the beauty of His presence continually.

It's one thing to grasp something, but it is sometimes another thing to live it! The Lord has shown us a more glorious way in Him, but often we feel the counter-attack instead. How do we live above it – above the stabbing hurts of the world? Come to Jesus, live in Him. We know that, but how? Lay it at His feet, or at the foot of the cross, lay it down, don't take it up again. Why is that hard? Why does the nagging pain of it, continue to gnaw at one? Pray, 'Lord, rid me of it, I don't want it. Forgive me for allowing it to gnaw at me. I am Yours and You are above all that.'

How did Jesus react to hurts? Perfectly. But how did He feel? Forgiving, understanding, with the Father's love. All this is available to us as well. Yes! Choose to forgive, forget, ask God to cleanse you with His love instead, to wash all the ugliness away with His embracing love. Thank You Lord, for it is done. We can now enter His presence with a new joy, a new peace, filled with His wonderful love.

Chapter 5

To Dwell in His Presence

There are differences between abiding and dwelling. The Oxford dictionary explains the meanings:

Abide – abode, remain, continue, adhere to, sustain, face. Enter – come in or into, the church takes orders, admission, enter, engage, agreement, sympathise with feelings, form part of a plan, assume possession or function to deal with.

Dwell – To keep one's attention fixed, prolong it, live in a specified place or state, dwell in secure.

The Bible says the same. To dwell in Him is a deeper level than abiding in Him as Psalm 91:1–2 says:

'He who dwells in the shelter of the Most High,
  who abides in the shadow of the Almighty,
will say to the LORD, "My refuge and my fortress;
  my God, in whom I trust."'

The Lord becomes our refuge and fortress in whom we can trust. In Him we find our security.

We will now come to the place where we look forward to our special times with Him daily, for we will find a new joy in His presence. We will see Him as bigger and more glorious than before. We will see Him as more real and will therefore guard ourselves to walk cleanly before Him at all times, for we will fear to hurt Him by any sin. We will want to be pleasing to Him even as Isaiah 33:5 says:

> 'The Lord is exalted, for he dwells on high;
>   He will fill Zion with justice and righteousness;
> and he will be the stability of your times,
>   abundance of salvation, wisdom, and knowledge;
>   the fear of the Lord is His treasure.'

This may be for a nation or individual, but in order to dwell in the Lord you will have to live in righteousness or you will not even be able to enter in, let alone to dwell in Him. This alone will cause a holy fear within and make us guard ourselves that no carnal fear may enter us to cut us off from our most high God. This will also cause us to repent quickly, for once we have tasted of the beauty of God's presence, we will not want anything to spoil it.

We will have a new hunger for the things of God. We will seek Him daily with our whole hearts as Psalm 27:4–5 says:

> 'One thing have I asked of the Lord,
>   that will I seek after;
> that I may dwell in the house of the Lord
>   all the days of my life,
> to behold the beauty of the Lord,
>   and to enquire in his temple.
> For he will hide me in his shelter in
>   the day of trouble;
> he will conceal me under the cover of his tent,
>   he will set me high upon a rock.'

Not only will we seek Him but we will find Him. At first this is not always very easy. It seems that He wants to test us, to find out how serious we really are to dwell in His presence. At first I managed to dwell in Him for two hours before coming out, then four hours as I went about the daily tasks of life. I remember going shopping and still feeling I was in His presence. I am speaking of a deeper level of His presence here.

After this I came to a place where I could walk in His presence for two days, before coming out of it and so it went on until I found the place of practising His presence daily without coming out of it and this is possible. I then realised the next section of Psalm 27:5 taking on a new meaning within me. When walking, as dwelling in the presence of our Lord, a new peace covers us, like a tent. Things that would have hurt us or worried us before just seem to bounce off us. They are no longer able to penetrate us or reach into our hearts. They just bounce off us as worthless, compared to the beauty and peace we now walk in. This also enables us to deal with problems that come our way, with wisdom and under-standing, with the justice and the righteousness of the Lord.

What does this enable us to do? Psalm 23:6 says:

> *'Surely goodness and mercy shall follow me*
> *all the days of my life;*
> *and I shall dwell in the house of the* LORD
> *for ever.'*

When we learn to dwell in the Lord's presence we become more and more positive, we become more and more joyful, we become stronger and stronger in our Lord. Psalm 84:4–6 says:

> *Blessed are those who dwell in thy house,*
> *ever singing thy praise!*

Blessed are the men whose strength is in thee,
in whose heart are the highways to Zion.
As they go through the valley of Baca
they make it a place of springs;
the early rain also covers it with pools.
They go from strength to strength;
the God of gods will be seen in Zion.'

The more we dwell in the Lord's presence the more we can walk in His strength. We can never be the same again, not when you meet with the beauty of His presence, for His presence changes you. Sometimes it is too holy to speak; you have to receive from Him, and hear Him speak to you. When I reached this stage of dwelling in Him, He said to me one day:

'I said to you once before, abide in Me and I shall surely abide in you. Now I am calling you to live in Me, My child, not just to visit, but to live in Me, to dwell in Me, to stay connected with Me at all times, for you shall have need of My presence and power at any time of day or night and I can only do My work through your life if you stay in constant communion with Myself. Yes, My child, seek My presence at all times and you shall not be disappointed.'

I was excited to respond to the Lord with this call to live in Him and the results have been amazing. Certainly I was never disappointed, but rather filled with ecstatic joy at what the Lord can do.

It is as if you take the joy of the Lord with you wherever you go and things just happen even as Psalm 84:6 says.

After speaking on Premier Radio about what happened in Malawi, we had rather an overwhelming response with phone calls from people who needed healing. The Lord healed a few of them over the phone, others I invited to join us for a healing weekend down in Kent.

Saturday in Kent was set aside for praying for the sick. It started at 10.30 a.m. and ended at 8.30 p.m. It was the longest I have ever prayed for people, also one of the most exciting. There were many healings, mostly arthritic pains, a lot of inner healing and a lot were baptised in the Holy Spirit. What was special was a very real presence of the Lord upon myself and six people who were called by God to move into the realm of healing and deliverance. They had come to learn how to pray for the sick and the Lord anointed them so much that they could barely hold back the tears because of His beautiful touch. As they prayed for people I watched the Lord heal them through their hands.

Towards the end of the service a man entered the church asking to be saved from violence and drunkenness. We led him to the Lord.

As we prayed for him he fell to the floor and shook and cried for half an hour. Then six teenagers walked into the church, saw the man shaking on the floor and asked, 'What's happening to him?'

'The Lord's dealing with him,' I replied.

'That's scary,' they answered.

'When he gets up,' I said, 'I will ask him to come and tell you himself what is happening to him.'

Minutes later he got up off the floor quite wobbly. I asked him to come and share what was happening to the teenagers. He did and he spoke straight facts about his old life, meeting with Jesus, and how Jesus had filled him with incredible love and peace and forgiveness as he lay on the floor. 'I will never and can never and never ever want to return to my old life again . . . not now I have met with Jesus.' He ended, 'I must go now. I have an appointment to go to,' and he was gone.

Two of the teenagers were biting back tears so I challenged

them all with a choice of continuing as they were or to receive Jesus. Four of them responded and accepted Jesus as their Lord and saviour. Next all six went up to the kneeling rail and knelt down and prayed.

The associate minister was amazed at what he saw and that was not all. The next morning I saw the man who had first come to Jesus in church with his partner, and daughter. After the service his partner and daughter also became Christians and the Lord also healed her right ear. They have now joined the church.

The people who had helped pray for the sick also had good reports as they went to their own churches on Sunday. Their pastors gave them opportunities to pray for the sick after the service and the people were healed.

The demonstration of God is shown through the healings, and as God's people pray for the sick more, or walk more in the different gifts of the Spirit that the Lord gives, they will go forward for Him, from strength to strength and people will see for themselves that it is Jesus that is doing it.

Chapter 6

For Him to Dwell in Us

As we give ourselves for the Lord each day so He gives of Himself to be with us. James 4:5–8 says:

> 'Or do you suppose that it is in vain that the scripture says, "He yearns jealously over the spirit which he has made to dwell in us"? But he gives more grace; therefore it says, "God opposes the proud, but gives grace to the humble." Subject yourselves therefore to God. Resist the devil and he will flee from you. Draw near to God and he will draw near to you. Cleanse your hands, you sinners, and purify your hearts, you men of double mind.'

For the Holy Spirit to dwell in our hearts, we have to be cleansed of any sin within us. No matter how close we come to the Lord, sin can still come up as an issue to be dealt with, for even the smallest sin can cut us off from the presence of God, until it is confessed and dealt with.

To be cut off from the presence of God will be terrible for us even for a short while. We will understand how Jesus felt when He cried out in Mark 15:34:

> 'And at the ninth hour Jesus cried with a loud voice, "Elo-i, Elo-i, lama sabachthani?" which means, "My God, my God, why hast thou forsaken me?"'

God could not look on Jesus while He was carrying the sin of the world upon Him, your sin, my sin. God is holy. He cannot look upon sin. We become separated from Him if we sin. Only what Jesus did for us on the cross can cleanse us from that sin. We have to return to the cross of Jesus in repentance, and receive His forgiveness, then we are set free to come back to His presence. We need to be careful not to grieve the Holy Spirit.

It may take time to regain the level you were walking in the Lord before. For this reason we ought to walk in the Lord very carefully, keeping our eyes open, thinking and praying, keeping clear from sin as we would from a plague. As James 4:7 says:

> *'Submit yourselves therefore to God. Resist the devil and he will flee from you.'*

If we resist the devil, God will dwell with us. As 2 Chronicles 6:18 says:

> *'But will God dwell indeed with man on the earth? Behold, heaven and the highest heaven cannot contain thee.'*

And Revelation 21:3–4 says:

> *'And I heard a loud voice from the throne saying, "Behold, the dwelling of God is with men. He will dwell with them, and they shall be his people, and God himself will be with them; he will wipe away every tear from their eyes, and death shall be no more, neither shall there be mourning nor crying nor pain anymore, for the former things have passed away."'*

But we still live in the former times. The second coming of **Jesus** has not yet occurred. These verses are speaking of heaven. The good news is that Jesus' first coming has already happened. After Jesus ascended into heaven He sent His Holy Spirit to dwell in our hearts. We are able to come into His glorious presence and we are able to live in His presence and the Holy Spirit can dwell in our hearts. We have already passed from death to life. We also become one of His people, we become connected with God and He becomes connected to us, for God's Spirit dwells in us.

1 Corinthians 3:16–17 says:

> *'Do you not know you are God's temple and that God's Spirit dwells in you? If any one destroys God's temple, God will destroy him. For God's temple is holy, and that temple you are.'*

Colin Urquhart gave a wonderful sermon on the temple within us and I have made it part of my life. He spoke first on the four pillars:

1. Holiness – we have to live a holy life clean from sin;
2. Faith – we have to live a life of faith in Jesus;
3. Love – we need to love God and through His love love one another;
4. Power – through living for Jesus, dying to self in order to live for others will release God's power through us in whatever gifts the Lord has given to us.

The temple also has a roof. We will call this truth, for we have to walk in full truth, for truth sets us free. The temple also has walls. The walls of wisdom keep outside what should be kept outside – all sin – and keep inside what should be kept inside – the presence of the Lord. The temple also has windows to let in the light of the Lord, full of glory. Here we meet God where the Holy of Holies lives, in constant communication with the Lord who will then enable our light to shine before men.

We also have senses. Eyes are the windows of our bodies, letting the light in. We must never let any darkness pollute this. Do not look at bad things as this will let darkness in, rather fix your eyes on Jesus. Only look on the positive things in life, on doing good. Ears, like eyes, can let darkness and negative things enter us if we listen to bad things, even gossip or unbelief. Don't listen to it. Be holy to the Lord. Then we have a mouth, a doorway to the overflow. Out of the heart the mouth speaks. We need to give account for every foolish word, for the power of the word is powerful. We should rather be as a fountain of life, to bless, encourage, forgive. Nothing negative should come out of our mouths. What we say should be holy, for God knows our words even before they are on our lips, for He discerns what is in the temple.

Through the Holy Spirit God is able to dwell in our hearts. Is this not worth everything? Is this not the most wonderful gift, the most wonderful potential for our lives, to have the Holy Spirit to dwell in our hearts every day of our lives? Is this not why Paul prays in Ephesians 3:14–19:

> *'For this reason I bow my knees before the Father, from whom every family in heaven and on earth is named, that according to the riches of his glory he may grant you to be strengthened with might through his Spirit in the inner man, and that Christ may dwell in your hearts through faith; that you, being rooted and grounded in love, may have power to comprehend with all the saints what is the breadth and length and height and depth, and to know the love of Christ which surpasses knowledge, that you may be filled with all the fullness of God.'*

To comprehend the love of God would take all eternity and then we only discover the beginning of it. The Lord gave me a tiny glimpse of His love some time ago. I had raised my voice in sharp rebuke towards my daughter and then realised this was not God's way.

I came to the Lord in repentance expecting a deserved rebuke but instead experienced His love and then He spoke to me these words:

> 'You are mine and I am doing a new thing in your life that will release you fully into My work. You need to spend much time in My love. You need to absorb My love deep deep within your heart, so much so that you become secure in My love, trust in My love, know My love.
>
> Then, My child, you will not turn away as unworthy from Me at every mistake you make, but shall run into My arms instead. For worthiness has nothing to do with love. Worthiness is of self-effort, of the world. But love, My child, is so much higher, so much stronger. Love is of Myself and this love, My child, you need to become so grounded in and secure that nothing will be able to shake it, nothing will be able to separate it.'

He then led me to Romans 8:35–39:

> *'Who shall separate us from the love of Christ? Shall tribulation, or distress, or persecution, or famine, or nakedness, or peril or sword? As it is written,*
> > *"For thy sake we are being killed all the day long;*
> > *we are regarded as sheep to be slaughtered."*
> *No, in all these things we are more than conquerors through him who loved us. For I am sure that neither death, nor life, nor angels, nor principalities, nor things present, nor things to come, nor powers, nor height, nor depth, nor anything else in all creation, will be able to separate us from the love of God in Christ Jesus our Lord.'*

This is unconditional love. This word made a powerful impact on me. Instead of a mistake, making me react out of fear, I can now react out of love. To do things out of love is the right motive. Because love is unearned, it makes one humble and keeps one humble. One realises deep within that it is only through the love and grace of Jesus that we have any hope at all. It is through Him alone and what He did for us on the cross, that we can have this glorious new life in Him and be partakers in His wonderful love, and have His precious Holy Spirit to dwell in our hearts. This also helped me to correct my daughter through love. John 14:15–21 says:

> *'If you love me, you will keep my commandments. And I will pray the Father, and he will give you another Counselor, to be with you for ever, even the Spirit of truth, whom the world cannot receive, because it neither sees him nor knows him; you know him, for he dwells with you, and will be in you. I will not leave you desolate; I will come to you. Yet a little while, and the world will see me no more, but you will see me; because I live, you will live also. In that day you will know that I am in my Father, and you in me, and I in you. He who has my commandments and keeps them, he it is who loves me; and he who loves me will be loved by my Father, and I will love him and manifest myself to him.'*

To receive the Holy Spirit daily within us we need to receive Him into our hearts, spirits, mind and body.

We need Jesus in our hearts and spirits, as we reach out into the boundless, touching the beauty of Jesus, discerning His nature, receiving His love, His joy, His peace. We need to receive Him into our minds, that He may dwell there, so that we will begin to see from His perspective, think as He would think, understand others as He would. His dwelling in our minds will change our emotions to love others with His love, and feel as He would feel. This is growing in Him, increasing our capacity to love and care and do.

We also need to receive Him into our bodies so that we can actively feel His presence reaching every area with the pulsating vibration of His life within – His cleansing, His indwelling, His power to walk in His ways.

As He dwells in us, we are able to hear His voice, speak forth His words and allow Him to touch and heal others through our hands.

Nine-year-old David gets out of his wheelchair and walks.
Clapping in her wheelchair behind him is seventeen-year-old Jennifer
who was next to stand up in the power of Jesus
(St Mary's Crusade, Malawi)

No unholiness can remain. Even sickness may leave if He really indwells to this extent and this is His will for us.

If we let God have His way in us, we will be transformed by the indwelling of His Holy Spirit within us.

Chapter 7

To Walk in the Light
of His Presence

John 8:12 says:

> *'Again Jesus spoke to them, saying, "I am the light of the world; he who follows me will not walk in darkness, but will have the light of life."'*

When we have the light of God's presence, the Holy Spirit living within us, we will have the light of life. If we have the light of life within us we can clearly see where we are going.

Just like a torch switched on, we can see the way through the darkness. But as the bulb in a torch has to be connected to the battery, we have to be connected to God. If any rust is between the light bulb and the battery the torch will not work. If there is any rust of sin in our lives, we to shall not be connected with God and we will walk in darkness.

Also a torch battery has to be replaced or recharged regularly, or the light will become dim and then go out completely. In the same way the battery of our hearts needs to be recharged by prayer in God's presence to keep His light. If we try and walk without prayer our light will become dim and then we will find ourselves walking in darkness, fumbling to find our way through a dark world. We will become empty with nothing to give out.

We need to come into the Lord's presence in prayer every day of our lives and the busier we are for Him, the more time in His presence is needed, not only to pray for our situations, but to rest in Him, to wait on Him to fill us and to prepare us for our daily walk in Him. Even as the Jews had to gather manna daily to eat in the wilderness on their way to the promised land, we have to eat our spiritual infilling from God daily on our way through life to our promised land of eternal life. Like the manna in the desert, yesterday's bread is no longer good enough for today, nor can we save today's bread for tomorrow. We have to eat of it every day of our lives as John 6:31–35 says:

> *'"Our fathers ate the manna in the wilderness; as it is written, 'He gave them bread from heaven to eat.'" Jesus then said to them, "Truly, truly, I say to you, it was not Moses who gave you the bread from heaven; my Father gives you the true bread from heaven. For the bread of God is that which comes down from heaven, and gives life to the world." They said to him, "Lord, give us this bread always." Jesus said to them, "I am the bread of life; he who comes to me shall not hunger, and he who believes in me shall never thirst."'*

We truly need to come to Jesus daily for our manna, the light of life. Only then can we serve God by bringing His light into our lives and into other people's lives, even as Jesus did in John 4:31–34:

> *'Meanwhile the disciples besought him, saying, "Rabbi, eat." But he said to them, "I have food to eat of which you do not know." So the disciples said to one another, "Has anyone brought him food?" Jesus said to them, "My food is to do the will of him who sent me, and accomplish his work."'*

We have to eat physical food to keep our bodies alive, to live out our lives on earth. In the same way we have to eat of the spiritual manna of God, so that His light may give us spiritual light to do His work on earth, to walk as His lights on this earth. It also says in Mathew 5:16:

> *'Let your light so shine before men, that they may see your good works and give glory to your father who is in heaven.'*

So how do we carry His light before men? First by knowing Jesus within us. 'But how,' we may ask, 'can we know someone whom we have never seen?' When we meet someone is it the looks that tell us who he is, or is it the character within the person that shines through him that tells us who he is? If it is only looks then we do not know that person. We need to know what is behind the face, how he thinks, how he looks at life, who he really is.

This is what Jesus has revealed to us of Himself, who He really is. He has revealed to us His love, His compassion, His character, His strength. All the fruit of the Holy Spirit shines through His countenance. When we come into His presence, we recognise Him by the beauty of His presence, His goodness, how He thinks, how He loves people, even how He feels. Is this not so much closer than just looking at a person?

When you spend a lot of time with a person, especially someone stronger than yourself, someone you look up to and respect, their character, world view, ideas and even dreams will rub off onto you. In the same way, when you spend much time in the presence of Jesus, His ways, His vision, His fruit, His love, His compassion will rub off into your own life and as you receive Him into your heart, His countenance, His beauty, His ways will shine through your life. More and more good works will be done so naturally out of His love alone without any effort or thought of your own.

These good works will have become part of you – who you are. Jesus in you will shine forth from you with all the qualities and fruit of the Holy Spirit. Simply by 'being in Jesus' you will be a witness to others to the beauty and character within that will change lives.

A Hindu lady was listening in the background to something on healing on the radio. As she was suffering from lymphoma, a cancer, for a year and a half, she began to listen more closely to me speaking on Premier Radio. She then took down the number to phone Lifeline and they gave her my phone number. I invited her to come to our Monday evening prayer meeting and gave her the phone number of others who were also driving up from London to attend the meeting and they gave her a lift. Six people from London arrived early, had supper with us and then joined us all in prayer. We prayed for a good two hours, as that night it seemed difficult to come into the Lord's presence.

First sitting, then standing, we persevered, until suddenly we broke through and the Lord's presence filled the room, causing each one of us to sink to our knees. After a while we began to minister to the sick and to each other. The presence of the Holy Spirit was so strong that even as we began to pray for someone the presence of the Lord took them to the floor and delivered them of things they needed deliverance from.

I walked up to the Hindu lady with cancer. As I lifted my hand to pray for her, she also fell to the ground and began to cry and cry as the Lord's presence touched her so deeply. Then she burst out in sheer joy as she received Jesus into her heart as her only true God, saying out loud that there was no other God and confessing openly to Him. Her joy was ecstatic for she had met with Jesus and got up to say so and also to say that she believed she was entirely healed. Eight days later she phoned me in great joy. She had visited the doctor that day and he confirmed what she already knew.

She has already joined a church and has bought a Bible for she is excited in her new found faith in Jesus.

We did not have to do a thing. The presence of Jesus in the room was sufficient for every healing, every deliverance, every need. His presence is sufficient and His presence in us is also sufficient for every need, if only we spend time with Jesus, if only we let Him radiate through our lives.

How do we let Him radiate through our lives? I asked the Lord this question one day: 'How is it, Lord, that some people have a greater anointing than others?'

The Lord replied, 'It is not the size of the anointing, but the degree to which you die to self to release the anointing that I give you.'

This revelation changed me. We can receive the anointing. This means that it is up to each one of us how much time we spend with Jesus to receive it and to how much we are prepared to die to self to release it.

So how do we die to self? It may be to die to our own self-consciousness to share, or to fears, or to wants. We may have to go where we do not wish to go, or sacrifice our time, or things, or money. We may have to struggle with our priorities, our plans or even our careers. The degree to which we are able to die to self – to our interests, to our desires or anything else that may get in the way – all depends on us and God's call on our lives.

As a riding instructor Saturday is a very booked up day with clients. I never went anywhere on a Saturday for 35 years, not even to a wedding. Then one day the Lord wanted me to go to an all-day conference. 'Lord, I can't go. It's on a Saturday.'

'What do you put first,' He challenged me, 'your business or My work?'

'You, of course,' I replied. Then on examining myself I realised I had put my business before God for 35 years. I repented and paid someone else to do that Saturday for me.

It was difficult to draw back at first and obey God. What if an accident occurred or the clients did not like a different instructor? The day went well. Then the Lord challenged me to do this once a month and I drew back more. Now I employ this same instructor and I am serving the Lord almost full time.

The riding school has not suffered for the Lord has blessed it and me, and the riding school continues to grow and prosper.

Now I truly put God first in my life above the business, above money spent on trips to spread the gospel, above searing heat, above having to sleep on the floor with rats, above everything. In fact any hardship I now see as a privilege. It is nothing compared to seeing the wonder of Jesus at work, to see Him heal the sick, set people free, answer their prayers, and to see them become Christians, to have the joy of serving Jesus. Most wonderful of all is the joy of knowing Him, and coming into His beautiful presence again and again until your heart is so full of His joy that it glows within with His glorious beauty and peace and a love so wonderful that all you want to do is to worship Him more and more and the more you do, the more He fills you with Himself.

It is then that things happen, for His Spirit is able to flow forth through you in power and healing, in ways greater than you could ever expect. When you reach this stage you find that indeed His light can shine even through your own life as you walk in His presence.

It was my third healing mission to Africa. There were three lame children in wheelchairs and Jesus healed all three as I prayed for them. It all just happened; first Mwawia, then David, then Jennifer. All three got out of their wheelchairs and walked. Only Jesus could do that. Mwawia did not want to get back into her wheelchair to go home. The next day she left the wheelchair at home and walked unaided with her mom to the crusade. David, who was nine years old, suddenly realising he could walk, became very over-active and ended up pushing his own wheelchair around at a run, radiating with sheer joy. I will never forget it, such incredible joy, as if Jesus was right there with us, for I felt His love for them and felt His joy. I felt as though I had flowed with Him in the miraculous and shared in His joy of seeing His children healed and set free.

To be part of something this glorious, to see Jesus at work in this way, is such a privilege. Such joy, such love. Jesus – our Master and King, Creator of heaven and earth.

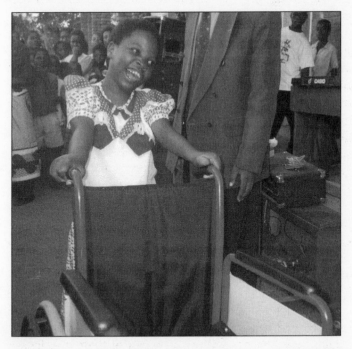

Mwawia had malaria five years ago and went into a coma for four months. She woke up paralysed and blind, but Jesus raised her from her wheelchair and completely healed her. Above she is pushing her own wheelchair in sheer delight (St Mary's Crusade, Malawi)

Chapter 8

Divine Communication

'O give thanks to the LORD, call on his name,
  make known his deeds among the peoples!
Sing to him, sing praises to him,
  tell of all his wonderful works!
Glory in his holy name;
  let the hearts of those who seek the LORD rejoice!
Seek the LORD and his strength,
  seek his presence continually!'   (Psalm 105:1–4)

The Bible tells us to call on the name of the Lord. Right from the beginning man has called on His name:

'To Seth also a son was born, and he called his name Enosh. At that time men began to call upon the name of the LORD.'
(Genesis 4:26)

Then others through the Bible also called upon His name:

'[Abram journeyed] to the place where he had made an altar at first; and there Abram called on the name of the LORD.'   (Genesis 13:4)

'Then Samson called to the Lord *and said, "O Lord* God, *remember me, I pray thee, and strengthen me, I pray thee . . . '*
(Judges 16:28)

'[Solomon said] then hear thou in heaven thy dwelling place, and forgive, and act, and render to each whose heart thou knowest, according to his ways (for thou, thou only, knowest the hearts of all the children of men).'   (1 Kings 8:39)

We have to call upon the name of the Lord from our hearts even as 2 Timothy 2:22 warns:

'So shun youthful passions and aim at righteousness, faith, love, and peace, along with those who call upon the name of the Lord from a pure heart.'

To call upon the name of the Lord it appears that the Lord first draws us to do so as in the Song of Solomon 1:4:

'Draw me after you, let us make haste . . . '

and Psalm 80:18:

'Then we will never turn back from thee;
  give us life, and we will call on thy name!'

Not only has man called on God but God has called on man. Again we can go right back to Exodus 3:4:

'When the Lord *saw that he turned aside to see, God called to him out of the bush, "Moses, Moses!" And he said, "Here am I." '*

and Exodus 19:20:

'And the Lord *came down upon Mount Sinai, to the top of the mountain; and the* Lord *called Moses to the top of the mountain, and Moses went up.'*

and 1 Samuel 3:4:

> *'Then the* Lord *called, "Samuel! Samuel!" and he said, "Here I am!"'*

God calls to man and man hears God and responds to Him. Now we have a two-way communication as we will see in Job:

> *'Then call, and I will answer;*
>   *or let me speak, and do thou reply to me.'*   (Job 13:22)

> *'Thou wouldest call, and I would answer thee.'* (Job 14:15)

This means sometimes the Lord will speak first. Once during the flight to South Africa while resting back in my seat the Lord said, 'Sit up. I want to speak to you.' I sat up and He encouraged me greatly. It was a wonderful time.

Many a person will ask, though, 'Why don't I hear God? How do I learn to hear God?' This question is answered in a prayer in Psalm 63:1–4:

> *'Oh God, thou art my God, I seek thee,*
>   *my soul thirsts for thee;*
> *my flesh faints for thee,*
>   *as in a dry and weary land where no water is.*
> *So I have looked upon thee in the sanctuary,*
>   *beholding thy power and glory.*
> *Because thy steadfast love is better than life,*
>   *my lips will praise thee.*
> *So I will bless thee as long as I live;*
>   *I will lift up my hands and call on thy name.'*

We have to put God first, to thirst for His presence as in a dry and weary land here on earth where no water of His presence is. Once we come into His presence where we can feel His love joy and peace within, where we can communicate with Him and hear Him speak to us, we will love and long for His presence more and more. We will also experience the beauty of His power and glory in His presence.

Only God's people will seek this presence, for the world does not know of it. The Lord will become our fortress and strength as Psalm 59:9–10:

> *'O my Strength, I will sing praises to thee,*
> *for thou, O God, art my fortress.*
> *My God in his steadfast love will meet me.'*

The Lord replies to our seeking Him, to our calling upon His name with promises from Jeremiah 33:2–3:

> *'Thus says the LORD who made the earth, the LORD who formed it to establish it – the LORD is his name: Call to me and I will answer you, and tell you great and hidden things which you have not known.'*

He promises to speak to us, to tell us of great and hidden things. He also promises to hear all who call upon Him in truth.

> *'The LORD is near to all who call upon him,*
> *to all who call upon him in truth.'*   (Psalm 145:18)

He also promises to protect us as He calls us to cleave to Him in love. This is very near to Him. It's where we receive His love and therefore we can also love Him as in Psalm 91:14–16:

> *'Because he cleaves to me in love, I will deliver him;*
> *I will protect him, because he knows my name.*

When he calls to me, I will answer him;
  I will be with him in trouble,
  I will rescue him and honour him.
With long life I will satisfy him,
  and show him my salvation.'

This scripture now brings us even closer to the Lord, for when we find the presence of God the devil can no longer find us and therefore no harm can come to us for we are in His presence. God's presence surrounds you and protects you as Psalm 91:3–5:

'For he will deliver you from the snare of the fowler
  and from the deadly pestilence;
he will cover you with his pinions,
  and under his wings you will find refuge;
  his faithfulness is a shield and buckler.
You will not fear the terror of the night,
  nor the arrow that flies by day,
nor the pestilence that stalks in darkness,
  nor the destruction that wastes at noonday.'

It is here that you can also come to know God more and more. As He trusts you He will allow you closer, even as you allow a friend you trust closer to you.

' "Now therefore, I pray thee, if I have found favour in thy sight, show me now thy ways, that I may know thee and find favour in thy sight. Consider too that this nation is thy people." And he said, "My presence will go with you, and I will give you rest." '　　　　　　　(Exodus 33:13–14)

Here Moses is asking God that he may know Him more, in a closer connection, a higher level, a deeper relationship. It was a longing of Moses' heart to know Him more and to be pleasing to God. Then God said, *'My presence will go with you, and I will give you rest.'*

This promise of God's presence going with you is very wonderful for now not only do you come into His presence in prayer, but His presence now stays with you and goes with you wherever you go. This in itself gives you a rest, for you know it is not you, but that it is God that is doing it.

The first time I came back from Africa, having seen about 250 healings by the Lord in Kenya, I wondered to myself, 'Will this work in England?'

Cirencester was my first invitation and I went along not knowing what would happen. Yet people still got healed. Then I was invited to Wantage and Jesus healed two people of cancer there. Yes, it did work. I then realised that the Holy Spirit and the presence of God came to these places with me, so I no longer had to worry, simply to rest in Jesus and let Him do it. My only, and important, preparation was prayer and waiting on God for His presence to fill me to overflowing, for serving God is not a project but an overflow. Waiting on God produces the overflow. If we read on in Exodus 33 from verse 15 we read the rest of the conversation that Moses had with the Lord:

> *'And he said to him, "If thy presence will not go with me, do not carry us up from here. For how shall it be known that I have found favour in thy sight, I and thy people? Is it not in thy going with us, so that we are distinct, I and thy people, from all other people that are upon the face of the earth?"'*
>
> (Exodus 33:15–16)

If His presence does not go with us, nothing will happen. It will not be worth going anywhere to pray for the sick or to exercise any other gift, for without God we can do nothing.

Only as we wait on God for His presence and anointing on our lives are we able to go with His presence. Also as Christians this is how we ought to walk, distinct in Christ, different from all other people that are upon the face of the earth, for God's presence can only go with God's people and no one else. In order for His presence to go with us, we have to put God first. Nothing must replace God, our hearts must be 100% His. If anything else, or any sin comes in, our walk with God comes to a stop and the enemy can then come to defeat us.

We must always draw near to God, then He will draw near to us. It is then that Isaiah 65:24 comes true:

> *'Before they call I will answer,*
> *while they are yet speaking I will hear.'*

I have actually seen this scripture come alive. One night as I prayed for people in Africa, some were getting healed even as I was about to lay hands on them and other people, waiting in line, were receiving healing even before I could pray for them. We will answer back to the Lord as in Psalm 116:1-2:

> *'I love the LORD, because he has heard*
> *my voice and supplications.*
> *Because he inclined his ear to me,*
> *therefore I will call on him as long as I live.'*

Love for God by the Holy Spirit is supernatural. It is far greater than any earthly love, to seek God and to keep on seeking Him daily:

> *'In the path of thy judgements,*
> *O LORD, we wait for thee;*
> *thy memorial name*
> *is the desire of our soul.*
> *My soul yearns for thee in the night,*
> *my spirit within me earnestly seeks thee.'*
>
> (Isaiah 26:8–9)

The more we find Him the more we want Him. Nothing on earth can compare with the glory of His presence. It is here we come to rest, it is here we come simply to appreciate His beauty, to absorb His heavenly love deep within our beings. It is here that He can change us, for His perfect love casts out all fear, His perfect love can bring deep inner healing, His perfect love can even cause us to cry with incredible joy. It is here God can say, *'Be still, and know that I am God'* (Psalm 46:10). Be still, so that everything is silenced. Wait until you are filled with God's presence, then words became inadequate. Your heart begins to talk instead with tears of joy, tears of love, tears of meeting with Him.

> *'Be silent before the Lord GOD!*
> *For the day of the LORD is at hand.'*   (Zephaniah 1:7)

> *'Be silent, all flesh, before the LORD; for he has roused himself*
> *from his holy dwelling.'*   (Zechariah 2:13)

Our silence moves God and activates His presence and glory. Our silence also enables us to hear the Lord speak to us.

> *'It stood still,*
> *but I could not discern its appearance.*
> *A form was before my eyes;*
> *there was silence, then I heard a voice:*
> *"Can mortal man be righteous before God?*
> *Can a man be pure before his maker?"'*   (Job 4:16–17)

This is where true prayer starts. His presence saturates your whole being until you feel like you are melting into Him, such a beautiful feeling. We find Him in the stillness of His presence, this divine connection with Him, and deeper and deeper levels await us, as we come into His presence.

It is also here that Isaiah 40:31 takes on a new meaning:

> *'but they who wait for the* Lord *shall renew their strength,*
> *they shall mount up with wings like eagles,*
> *they shall run and not be weary,*
> *they shall walk and not faint.'*

That is what prayer is like. It's almost like the time I released a wild bird that got trapped in the house and saw him rise in joy and relief up into the heavenlies in new-found freedom.

The tame bird knows nothing of the great outdoors. He is content to be a captured bird for he knows no better. So with thousands of people, they are content to live on this earth, not knowing the release, the joy, the freedom that prayer gives you, as you soar up high into the glorious presence of God, the expanse of His greatness, the beauty of His love, the expression of His great joy, the horizons of His indwelling peace.

Once one knows the greatness and beauty of God's love, never again will you want to be without it, never again will you want to be trapped by the limits of the world, for like the bird you will have found the vastness of the universe in Him.

Chapter 9

Holy Fire

'But when the king came in to look at the guests, he saw there a man who had no wedding garment; and he said to him, "Friend, how did you get in here without a wedding garment?" And he was speechless. Then the king said to the attendants, "Bind him hand and foot, and cast him into the outer darkness; there men will weep and gnash their teeth." For many are called, but few are chosen.'

(Mathew 22:11–14)

This is a hard word that Jesus is saying through the parable, so let us look up what Jesus is saying about garments.

'Let your garments be always white; let not oil be lacking on your head.' (Ecclesiastes 9:8)

We see here that this could be speaking of walking in righteousness with the oil of the Holy Spirit upon you.

Let's now look at the book of Revelation 16:15:

'Lo, I am coming like a thief! Blessed is he who is awake, keeping his garments that he may not go naked and be seen exposed!'

What does ' *be seen exposed'* mean here? It can only mean that the Lord's cloak of righteousness of white can cover any confessed sin that would be exposed and Revelation 3:2–5 explains this in even more depth:

> *'Awake, and strengthen what remains and is on the point of death, for I have not found your works perfect in the sight of my God. Remember then what you received and heard; keep that, and repent. If you will not awake, I will come like a thief, and you will not know at what hour I will come upon you. Yet you still have a few names in Sardis, people who have not soiled their garments; and they shall walk with me in white, for they are worthy. He who conquers shall be clad thus in white garments, and I will not blot his name out of the book of life; I will confess his name before my Father and before his angels. He who has ear, let him hear what the Spirit says to the churches.'*

So a soiled garment is him who is soiled by sin and a white garment means righteousness.

> *'I put on righteousness, and it clothed me;*
> *my justice was like a robe and a turban.*
> *I was eyes to the blind,*
> *and feet to the lame.*
> *I was a father to the poor,*
> *and I searched out the cause of him whom I did not*
> *know.'*   (Job 29:14–16)

'I put on righteousness, and it clothed me.' We have no righteousness without Jesus who forgives us and clothes us with His presence.

The more we allow the Lord to cleanse us, the more He will free us to be clothed in righteousness. That is, we do not only ask the Lord to free us from sin, but to free us from self as

well. The **me** and the **I** also have to die, in order to release
Him through us. In allowing the Lord to do this within
us, we become clothed in righteousness, for His love and
compassion has replaced the **me** and the **I** within us and we
begin to care for others more, becoming eyes for the blind,
feet for the lame, a father to the poor.

> *'But let justice roll down like waters,*
> *and righteousness like an ever-flowing stream.'*
>
> (Amos 5:24)

This reminds me of John 7:37–38:

> *'If any one thirst, let him come to me and drink. He who*
> *believes in me, as the scripture has said, "Out of his heart*
> *shall flow rivers of living water."'*

We have to come to the Lord and drink of His living
waters, His presence, His righteousness. Only then is it
possible to be clothed with the right garments for heaven,
as verse 39 goes on to say:

> *'Now this he said about the Spirit, which those who believed*
> *in him were to receive; for as yet the Spirit had not been given,*
> *because Jesus was not yet glorified.'*

John the Baptist said in Mathew 3:11:

> *'I baptise you with water for repentance, but he who is*
> *coming after me is mightier than I, whose sandals I am not*
> *worthy to carry; he will baptise you with the Holy Spirit and*
> *with fire.'*

He does not say only with the Holy Spirit, but also with fire.
Let's read Acts 2:1–4:

'When the day of Pentecost had come, they were all together in one place. And suddenly a sound came from heaven like the rush of a mighty wind, and it filled all the house where they were sitting. And there appeared to them tongues as of fire, distributed and resting on each one of them. And they were all filled with the Holy Spirit and began to speak in other tongues, as the Spirit gave them utterance.'

Let's look at two more scriptures about fire:

'And the angel of the Lord *appeared to him in a flame of fire out of the midst of a bush; and he looked, and lo, the bush was burning, yet it was not consumed.'*   (Exodus 3:2)

'Therefore let us be grateful for receiving a kingdom that cannot be shaken, and thus let us offer to God acceptable worship, with reverence and awe; for our God is a consuming fire.'   (Hebrews 12:28–29)

The bush was burning but not consumed, and our God is a consuming fire. What does this mean? This is answered very well in 1 Corinthians 3:10–16:

'According to the grace of God given to me, like a skilled master builder I laid a foundation, and another man is building upon it. Let each man take care how he builds upon it. For no other foundation can any one lay than that which is laid, which is Jesus Christ. Now if any one builds on the foundation with gold, silver, precious stones, wood, hay, straw – each man's work will become manifest; for the Day will disclose it, because it will be revealed with fire, and the fire will test what sort of work each one has done. If the work which any man has built on the the foundation survives, he will receive a reward. If any man's work is burned up, he will suffer loss, though he himself will be saved, but only as

through fire. Do you not know that you are God's temple and that God's Spirit dwells in you?'

This means that His holy fire will only burn up the chaff of sin in our lives and will refine the good within us but will not consume us. Like the burning bush it will burn within us without consuming us. Only the negative things within us shall be burned up, if we yield ourselves to Him to do this.

When we are touched by His holy fire, the fire will not burn us up. The fire will instead burn up the straw and stubble within us and refine us to be like gold. This will continue until our characters are transformed into the image of Jesus.

The more time we spend in the presence of God, the more His holy flame is able to do His wondrous work within us, penetrating into every area of our heart and life, bringing to the surface things that need dealing with, healing the inner hurts of the past and bringing His life in abundance to every area of our life and ministry. Spending much time in the presence of God is therefore the most worthwhile time that you can spend on this earth.

His indwelling presence is heavenly for He is sent from heaven to dwell in our earthly bodies. Therefore to constantly dwell in His presence keeps you in eternal contact with heaven, making it possible to bring heaven down on earth, as you do His will on earth as it is done in heaven. As in the Lord's prayer, thy kingdom come, *'thy will be done, on earth, as it is in heaven.'* This means God can do His will on earth, through us.

'Many are called, but few are chosen.' Is this because the refiner's fire of the Holy Spirit must first refine us, before He can choose us, before we can become His chosen? This is again answered by Scripture in Isaiah 6:4–9:

'And the foundations of the thresholds shook at the voice of him who called, and the house was filled with smoke. And I

*said: "Woe is me! For I am lost; for I am a man of unclean
lips, and I dwell in the midst of a people of unclean lips; for
my eyes have seen the King, the LORD of hosts!" Then flew
one of the seraphim to me, having in his hand a burning coal
which he had taken with tongs from the altar. And he
touched my mouth, and said: "Behold, this has touched your
lips; your guilt is taken away, and your sin forgiven." And I
heard the voice of the Lord saying, "Whom shall I send, and
who will go for us?" Then I said, "Here am I! Send me." And
he said, "Go and say to this people . . . " '*

We see here that, yes, the refiner's fire must first refine us. We
can then become one of God's chosen.

There is one more point to add to the results of coming
through the refiner's fire. Jesus went into the wilderness
baptised in the Holy Spirit; He came out of the wilderness full of the Holy Spirit, ready for His miraculous ministry
ahead.

The refiner's fire causes a brokenness within us as we open
our hearts to want more and more of God's presence and
love. It is realising that we no longer want to live outside His
presence. We want to come to Him more and more. The Lord
becomes first in every area of our lives. We hunger and seek
for His presence daily. We become clothed in His garments
of righteousness and the oil of the Holy Spirit will not be
lacking in our lives.

> *'Thou hast said, "Seek ye my face."*
> *My heart says to thee,*
> *"Thy face, LORD, do I seek." '*   (Psalm 27:8)

Chapter 10

To Be Chosen by Him

There is no higher calling on our lives than to be chosen by God, and yet we were chosen before the foundation of the world. It was God's highest intention for us to become His chosen. But not all of us have realised this, not all of us are living up to the ideals that God intended for us before the foundation of the world. We have instead been trapped by earthly callings and have been content to live on a lower level than God intended.

> 'Blessed be the God and Father of our Lord Jesus Christ, who has blessed us in Christ with every spiritual blessing in the heavenly places, even as he chose us in him before the foundation of the world, that we should be holy and blameless before him. He destined us in love to be his sons through Jesus Christ, according to the purpose of his will.'
>
> (Ephesians 1:3–5)

Is this not sad, that many of us are not living at the level that God intended, that we have not received His love to be His sons and daughters through Jesus to be His chosen people?

> *'For you are a people holy to the* LORD *your God; the* LORD
> *your God has chosen you to be a people for his own*
> *possession, out of all the peoples that are on the face of the*
> *earth.'*   (Deuteronomy 7:6)

This was spoken to God's chosen people, the Jews, but
they did not live up to their calling and neither have we. We
have all fallen short of the glory of God, we have all walked
our own way, every one. Only through what Jesus did for us
on the cross have a few of us, Jew and Gentile, realised our
calling, followed after God and become one of His chosen
people:

> *'chosen and destined by God the Father and sanctified by*
> *the Spirit for obedience to Jesus Christ and for sprinkling with*
> *his blood: May grace and peace be multiplied to you.'*
>   (1 Peter 1:2)

We have to come to God through the cross, Jew and
Gentile alike. Only through the blood of Jesus can we enter
in and become the chosen of God. We also have to be
sanctified, cleansed, refined by fire to become obedient.
Sometimes, if not always, people in whom God releases His
anointing have to go through a time of testing first.

Jesus spent 40 days in the wilderness before He began His
ministry. Moses spent 40 years in the wilderness before God
spoke to Him out of the burning bush. David began his
service after being a shepherd boy. Paul also spent time in
the wilderness.

It is the wilderness experience that prepares us for God's
work. It is there that the holy fire of God purges us from sin
and refines us like gold for the Lord to choose us and use us.

> *'Put on then, as God's chosen ones, holy and beloved,*
> *compassion, kindness, lowliness, meekness, and patience,*

forbearing one another and, if one has a complaint against another, forgiving each other; as the Lord has forgiven you, so you also must forgive. And above all these put on love, which binds everything together in perfect harmony. And let the peace of Christ rule in your hearts, to which indeed you were called in the one body.' (Colossians 3:12–15)

We have to put on these good qualities not only in prayer, but in our everyday life which is not always quite so easy.

It is always interesting that God always calls us His chosen, His beloved, and so we are if only we will receive His love.

A Hindu lady came to our prayer meeting. Jesus revealed Himself to her and healed her of lymphoma (a cancer). She became a Christian and has joined a church.

When we receive His love every day, it becomes easier to live out compassion, kindness, lowliness, meekness, patience, and forgiveness, for all these things come out of love for God and one another. The love of God enables us to live as His chosen people.

> *'For we know, brethren beloved by God, that he has chosen you; for our gospel came to you not only in word, but also in power and in the Holy Spirit and with full conviction.'*
>
> (1 Thessalonians 1:4–5)

The Word of God is living and active and when we share our faith with others, it, too, is living and active and His Word will not return void. When we do the work that God has chosen for us to do, that work will be effective for it cannot be other than effective. If we have heard God and follow Him in obedience, that work will succeed.

Peter says:

> *'But you are a chosen race, a royal priesthood, a holy nation, God's own people, that you may declare the wonderful deeds of him who called you out of darkness into his marvellous light.'*
>
> (1 Peter 2:9)

Chapter 11

To Be Loved by Him

It was a Saturday evening. I saw a vision of many many black people in a large tent all hungry for God, hands raised to receive Him. I felt I had heard God say, 'Speak simply and I will meet them where they are.' I thought, 'I must respond to Him and go.' Never yet had I ever spoken in any place other than a church. Little did I know then that this vision was to come true soon, but the Lord had much to teach me, much to show me and to start right then and there is just like God. He is a 'now' God, for He lives outside time so His time is the now, everlasting now.

It was good to come into His presence, to rest at His glorious feet. I felt well stretched that evening having taught all day and driven back from Paris the day before. To come into His glorious presence: I live for this, for when His presence touches you He makes you whole, full, content and full of joy.

I wrote, 'That He should come to meet us here.' Why did I write this down? To savour His presence longer, to remember it, in case He may speak to me. 'Is this okay?' I asked.

I felt the Lord answer me, 'Yes, and I will speak to you, for you are no longer your own, for you are no longer to make your own decisions or go your own way, but to seek Me and My way.'

'Please guide me, Lord. Which way do You wish me to go?' I replied.

'All I have asked of you is to spend time in My presence. I need to prepare you and then I will speak to you and guide you. Learn to wait on Me, then you shall also move with Me.'

'Yes,' I responded, in awe. 'I also know there is sacrifice in serving. Sorry I talk too much.'

'True strength comes from Me, not yourself. That is why you get tired. Learn to draw on My strength and that only comes when you spend time with Me. You also need to learn to love My people with My heart and you can only do this when you draw close to My heart. Do this now.'

I did and felt I was no longer my own. I belonged to God. His heart is far greater than mine, with rivers of compassion and love for His people flowing from it. I have no heart compared to His, I have to draw on His, to even begin to think of it.

> *'And he said to him, "You shall love the Lord your God with all your heart, and with all your soul, and with all your mind. This is the great and first commandment. And a second is like it, You shall love your neighbour as yourself. On these two commandments depend all the law and the prophets."'*
> (Matthew 22:37–40)

On Monday morning I went down to have breakfast and the Lord said, 'Put it back. You will be going on a fast.'

'OK, Lord.' I put the cereal back and spent the day with the Lord.

It was on Tuesday morning, the second day of the fast, that I spoke to the Lord saying, 'Lord, no one else has ever spoken to me like You do; such glorious words, such wisdom, such gentleness.'

Then He said, 'For it is I that created you. No one else can have the love for what He has created, other than the

Creator, and you are receiving this love, therefore you are able to also live it. Yes, you are mine and as you receive the workings of My hand upon your life, so you shall be able to absorb even more of My love and radiate even more of My love also towards My people, whom I have also created.'

On Tuesday evening I spoke with the Lord again. 'The incredible joy of knowing You, to feel Your love well deep within and feel that somehow You even love me. How can this be, Lord Jesus?'

And He answered, 'For this I created you, for as I walked with Adam and Eve in the garden, so too I walk and talk with you. I created man for a love relationship with Myself, but few have found it. I rejoice in you, My child, that you are finding it, for I am truly a God of love.'

'This is so glorious,' I replied.

He said, 'I will show you even more. Absorb My love, My child, for I love you and want you to receive My love.'

I responded, 'This is like a touch of heaven. You have touched me, Lord, and I feel I have touched You. Never have I ever felt such incredible love, not ever.'

He then said, 'My love is greater than any love the world has ever known. It is a love I have reserved for My children as they seek Me. Yes, My child, and you have received it. This produces **incredible heavenly joy**.'

On the third day of the fast, Wednesday, I woke up excited. The incredible joy still within me contrasted with the background noise of the world. I came straight back into His glorious, incredible, wonderful presence, experiencing a new dimension of worship – that of a pouring out something like incense into a misted pool before Him. I came into a holy silence. It was like being in two worlds at once, spiritually closer to Jesus than ever before, yet aware of the world around.

I heard Him speak, 'So is your worship before Me as the ointment poured forth on My feet by Mary. Yes, My child, there are also two dimensions of worship, that of worship at My feet and also that of worship in action in the world that you live in. That of serving My people comes out of your worship in My presence. Worship is likened to a giving out of yourself, a giving out of love, to Me. Worship is also a giving out of yourself to others for My sake in leading them to Myself and serving them. Both I receive as worship unto Myself.'

I felt I was receiving the life-changing ointment of His love and Holy Spirit within me. Yes, I needed a lot of changing and I wanted the Lord to change me. I felt His love seeping into my mind and thinking, into my ideas and values and I yielded to it. It was as pure gold, more precious than anything I had ever encountered. I realised that my relationship with God was far more important than anything I could do for Him, for out of our relationship with God is the essence of life and ministry. There is no joy more glorious, nothing better than the Lord communicating to us His precious truths into our spirits. Nothing could compare with His love.

'This is not fasting, this is feasting. I am overwhelmed with Your joy and Your love. I can barely contain it,' I said to the Lord.

He replied and said, 'This is My pleasure to give you My love. Receive it, My child, for it will change you. It shall renew you and it shall energise new life in My service. It will flow naturally and easily, for My love shall radiate through you, without effort of yourself. You shall simply yield to Me and I shall do it. You shall become an open channel of My love for this is the ministry that I will bless you with.'

'To live by Your love? You are transforming me. I need to find strength daily in Your love to do it,' I thought.

'For the love of Christ controls us, because we are convinced that one has died for all; therefore all have died. And he died

*for all, that those who live might live no longer for themselves
but for him who for their sake died and was raised.'*
(2 Corinthians 5:14–15)

*'and hope does not disappoint us, because God's love has
been poured into our hearts through the Holy Spirit which has
been given to us.'*
(Romans 5:5)

*'As the Father has loved me, so have I loved you; abide in my
love.'*
(John 15:9)

*'I in them and thou in me, that they may become perfectly
one, so that the world may know that thou hast sent me and
hast loved them even as thou hast loved me.'* (John 17:23)

On Thursday, the fourth day of the fast, the Lord called me
into His glorious presence. The scriptures of yesterday were
confirmed and I was encouraged by what the Lord did for me
yesterday. The spoken word and written word had become
one in my heart, the reality of our living God.

I tried to pray for other things, but seemed to rather get
caught up in worship and filled with incredible joy. He had
touched my heart and it was burning with great joy.

Again the Lord spoke: 'For this I have called you and yes, I
am doing a new thing in your heart. I am preparing you for
My service, for how can you serve Me if you do not know
Me? How can you proclaim that which you have not
experienced? Only contact with Myself can prepare you,
can energise you, can teach you, can equip you, for it is I that
will send you out and no other. As you go out empowered by
My Spirit, then you will see results, not as a result of your
ministry, but as a result of My workings through your life.
You are to become a channel of My love and power to My
people whom I also love. Only as you give yourself to Me in
total love and trust can I fill you with My beauty to then give

out to others. All other needs will just fall into place. Come unto Me, My child, and receive of My love.'

> *'Jesus answered him, "If a man loves me, he will keep my word, and my Father will love him, and we will come to him and make our home with him. He who does not love me does not keep my words; and the word which you hear is not mine but the Father's who sent me. These things I have spoken to you, while I am still with you. But the Counselor, the Holy Spirit, whom the Father will send in my name, he will teach you all things, and bring to your remembrance all that I have said to you. Peace I leave with you; my peace I give to you; not as the world gives do I give to you. Let not your hearts be troubled, neither let them be afraid. You heard me say to you, 'I go away, and I will come to you.' If you loved me, you would have rejoiced, because I go to the Father; for the Father is greater than I.'"*   (John 14:23–28)

This scripture suddenly meant so much to me for I felt that I had been with Jesus and He was now bringing the fast to an end and I didn't want it to end. I also didn't want to lose that glorious contact with Him. I felt like crying at the ending of the fast – or had it been more a feast?

Then He said, 'Go, My child, for I am with you always. You need to move out now, but know that I move out with you. I am still with you and I will still reveal myself to you, for this love relationship with you is only the beginning. I have much more in store for you, My child, and that is why you also love Me.'

Anybody can have a love relationship with the Lord. That is why I have shared with you these special four days of fasting. With each of us He will reveal himself differently, for we are all so different in personalities and callings. To some He will share Himself through pictures, or visions, or ideas. He does not have to reveal Himself through words as He did for me. For some people He may simply reveal Himself to them in silence. Each way the Lord reveals Himself to us is as precious as the other and as meaningful to each individual.

Yes, this fast was a beautiful four days with Jesus, but it has not stopped there, it has carried on and His words to me have already come true in my life, which further confirms to me that I did hear Him speak to me and those four days were very real, very life-changing and have produced much fruit in my life. Though I have been criticised about hearing God, and you may be criticised as well, we need to look at the fruit in our lives. All I know is it is as biblical to hear God as it is to speak to Him, which is why I wrote the chapter on 'Divine Communication' and included many scriptures.

The other joy of hearing God speak to you is that it confirms Scripture. If it does not, then those words are not of God. It also makes the Word personal for us and encourages us so greatly. I have only shared with you my four day fast, as an example of hearing God, responding to Him, growing in Him and deepening our relationship with Him.

There are many more scriptures on love. Here are some others that the Lord showed me during those four days:

> *'See what love the Father has given us, that we should be called children of God.'* (1 John 3:1)

> *'Therefore be imitators of God, as beloved children. And walk in love, as Christ loved us and gave himself up for us, a fragrant offering and sacrifice to God.'* (Ephesians 5:1)

> *'And it is my prayer that your love may abound more and more, with knowledge and all discernment, so that you may approve what is excellent, and may be pure and blameless for the day of Christ, filled with the fruits of righteousness which come through Jesus Christ, to the glory and praise of God.'*
> (Philippians 1:9–10)

'but showing steadfast love to thousands of those who love me and keep my commandments.'   (Deuteronomy 5:10)

'To him who loves us and has freed us from our sins by his blood.   (Revelation 1:5)

'Yea, he loved his people;
  all those consecrated to him were in his hand;
so they followed in thy steps,
  receiving direction from thee.'   (Deuteronomy 33:3)

When we obey His commandments and live our lives in obedience to Him, then we receive even more of His love.

'he will love you, bless you, and multiply you.'
          (Deuteronomy 7:13)

'But, as it is written,
  "What no eye has seen, nor ear heard,
  nor the heart of man conceived,
  what God has prepared for those who love Him."'
          (1 Corinthians 2:9)

'I will most gladly spend and be spent for your souls. If I love you the more, am I to be loved the less?'
          (2 Corinthians 12:15)

'for the Father himself loves you, because you have loved me and have believed that I came from the Father.'
          (John 16:27)

'But if one loves God, one is known by him.'
          (1 Corinthians 8:3)

'But God, who is rich in mercy, out of the great love with which he loved us.'   (Ephesians 2:4)

When we spend more and more time in and receiving God's love, it enables us to walk in love until we can say like Paul in Galatians 2:20:

> *'I have been crucified with Christ; it is no longer I who live, but Christ who lives in me; and the life I now live in the flesh I live by faith in the Son of God, who loved me and gave himself for me.'*

When we are filled up with the love of God we will walk differently, we will think differently. God's love and compassion will give us a new understanding for people, a new patience, more kindness. We will walk with a new meekness and lowliness produced by His greatness. The more I know Him and His wonderful works that I see Him do, the more I want to get down to the floor in worship and awe. I see Him as greater and greater. The way He is in control of all things, He enables us to make the right contacts to help others. He heals, sets free, delivers people, with just so much love and compassion. He takes us at our word and even uses us to bless others. Yes and more, for it is not how much we know or who we are that matters, only that we are available and willing. God will use anyone who will make themselves available and who is willing to obey. His love changes us into His beloved people. His love enables all of us to become conquerors in this world of ours. God's love connects us to God, which no one can ever separate us from.

> *'No, in all these things we are more than conquerors through him who loved us. For I am sure that neither death, nor life, nor angels, nor principalities, nor things present, nor things to come, nor powers, nor height, nor depth, nor anything else in all creation, will be able to separate us from the love of God in Christ Jesus our Lord.'* (Romans 8:37–39)

It is then that we can live out this great love for others, for it is not how much we do, but the amount of love with which we do it. It is not how much we live out our life for God, but rather the love that God is able to live out through us. It is one thing to receive God's love within, it is another thing to live out God's love towards others.

Yes, we want God's love to fill our hearts, but do we want to love others with it? God pours His love into our hearts, that we may also pour out God's love towards others. Therefore as we receive God's love, a dying to self has also to take place, that His love for others may also take place. So we receive God's love. We let it saturate us, until we live in it twenty-four hours a day. His love begins to break down our hard crusts. It begins to melt our ice-clad hearts. It begins to soften our world taught minds, until it can even show through our eyes in tears, until it changes us into a true child of God, who can feel as He would feel, see as He would see, do as He would do.

Suddenly our priorities have changed. We become so full of the love of God and also love for others, that we become fully His and the outworking of His love becomes part of us, natural, normal, a pleasure, a joy.

We shall become joined to Him with everlasting cords of love, invisible yet stronger than steel. These cords of love that God may have with millions of people in heaven and on earth bind us to Him for all eternity; nothing can ever separate us (Romans 8:38–39). They also give us access to Him in undivided attention, even as you would connect to a friend with a mobile phone.

> *'They shall ask the way to Zion, with faces turned toward it, saying, "Come, let us join ourselves to the LORD in an everlasting covenant which will never be forgotten."'*
>
> (Jeremiah 50:5)

> *'I led them with cords of compassion,*
>   *with the bands of love.'*   (Hosea 11:4)

Through these cords of compassion, bands of love, we become united to Him as in 1 Corinthians 6:17:

> *'But he who is united to the Lord becomes one spirit with him.'*

First we join ourselves to the Lord then He leads us with cords of compassion, with bands of love, then we become united to Him, becoming as one spirit with Him. Then He goes even further in Hosea 2:19–20:

> *'And I will betroth you to me forever; I will betroth you to me in righteousness and in justice, in steadfast love, and in mercy. I will betroth you to me in faithfulness; and you shall know the LORD.'*

Chapter 12

New Life in Him

It is not just preparation, it is living in preparation all the time, ready. It is not spending hours binding Satan, it is living in God's strength against Satan. It is living in Him continually. Then regardless of the size of work God calls us to we are ready in Him. For it is Christ who does it. He has to do what we cannot do. We cannot heal the sick, some of us cannot even speak in public, but He can do it all and does do it.

So what is this new life in Christ? This is what we receive from God in our meeting place with God, holy, dedicated, set apart, where the river of life may fill us and then flow out of us into the world and even out to the nations of the world through us.

This is the supernatural power and anointing. This life may flow through us from God. This life may take us to far or near places. We will be able to take His life and anointing with us and we will do things we have never dreamed of, because the anointing will be upon us to enable wonderful things to happen.

Let us first look up 'life' in the dictionary:

Life – the active principle peculiar to animals, plants and common to them all, is the presence or possession of life in or by the individuals. It's a living state, the time for which it lasts, or the part of this between its beginning or its end and the present, living things and their movements, energy or other characteristics manifest and influence, the manner of existence or written story of them, the business and pleasures of the world.

It also can escape death. There is the body in the natural world and the other life in the future – the conscious existence of the soul after death – immortal, eternal, everlasting, state of bliss, salvation after death.

This is an amazing explanation of life out of a worldly dictionary.

So life is both bodily life and also eternal life given by God to dwell in us, to enrich and enhance, to bring God's life into us and through us in life, power, healing and vitality. When His life supercedes our lives, He can then live His life through our lives. That is when God's healings, deliverance and power over evil can begin to operate through our mortal lives.

Living in God continually, by giving ourselves up to Him in prayer and inviting Him to dwell in our lives, continually enables His life to come into our lives and cause His life to flow out through us.

Let us now see what the Bible says, starting with Revelation 22:17:

> *'The Spirit and the Bride say, "Come.' And let him who hears say, "Come." And let him who is thirsty come, let him who desires to take the water of life without price.'*

'The Spirit and the Bride say, "Come."' This is an invitation from the Holy Spirit Himself and is open to all who would find life in Him. The invitation is for the water of life,

priceless and without price and anyone who is thirsty for it, may come.

> *'And he who sat upon the throne said, "Behold, I make all things new." Also he said, "Write this, for these words are trustworthy and true." And he said to me, "It is done! I am the Alpha and the Omega, the beginning and the end. To the thirsty I will give from the fountain of water of **life** without payment. He who conquers shall have this heritage, and I will be his God and he shall be my son."'* (Revelation 21:5–6)

Again He speaks of the water of life without payment. We can receive this water of life by simply coming to Him in prayer. God is the beginning and the end; from Him the living water flows.

> *'He who has an ear, let him hear what the Spirit says to the churches. To him who conquers I will grant to eat of the tree of life, which is in the paradise of God.'* (Revelation 2:7)

He speaks of the tree of life. Is this not where all life started in Genesis? But we have to be conquerors in order to eat of it, just like we have to be conquerors to receive the water of life, conquerors over sin and all the temptations and tricks of the devil. 2 Corinthians 4:10–12 says:

> *'always carrying in the body the death of Jesus, so that the life of Jesus may also be manifested in our bodies. For while we live we are always given up to death for Jesus' sake, so that the **life of Jesus** may be manifested in our mortal flesh. So death is at work in us, but life in you.'*

We must carry the death of Jesus within us, so that we may also carry His resurrected life within us also, for Christ becomes the life to all those who are dead to sin:

> *'who has made us competent to be ministers of a new*
> *covenant, not in a written code but in the Spirit; for the*
> *written code kills, but the Spirit gives life.'*
>
> (2 Corinthians 3:6)

The letter of the law condemns everyone, but those who
are dead to sin are given life in Christ by the Holy Spirit.

> *'For we are the aroma of Christ to God among those who are*
> *being saved and among those who are perishing, to one a*
> *fragrance from death to death, to the other the fragrance from*
> *life to life.'*   (2 Corinthians 2:15–16)

The Holy Spirit moves us from life to life, from one level of
life to a higher level of life, unifying the temporal life with
the eternal life. Those who live in God therefore become a
sweet aroma because they show forth His true life.

> *'but these are written that you may believe that Jesus is the*
> *Christ, the Son of God, and that believing you may have* **life**
> **in his name***.'*   (John 20:31)

True belief in Christ is **life**.

> *'Jesus said to him, "I am* **the way***, and* **the truth***, and* **the**
> **life***; no one comes to the Father, but by me."'* (John 14:6)

> *'Jesus said to her, "I am* **the resurrection and the life***; he*
> *who believes in me, though he die, yet shall he live, and he*
> *who* **lives** *and believes in me shall never die. Do you believe*
> *this?"'*   (John 11:25)

He is **the resurrection**. He is of God, in God and God,
therefore. **All life** is renewed from the Father through the
Son by the Holy Spirit.

> *'The thief comes only to steal and kill and destroy; I came that they may have **life**, and have it abundantly.'*
>
> (John 10:10)

Here Jesus is speaking of **life in Him**, eternal life as well as physical life. The thief, the devil, comes to steal, kill and destroy through sickness of the body or mind or through temptation, problems, hurts and many other things. Jesus came to give us life, health, and new life in Him. Christ is patient. He waits till we ask Him to enter to bring us His life. Through His life in us He is able to change us into His likeness. Through His anointing, as we spend time in His presence, we come closer to God and closeness to God enables Him to work in and through our lives to others. Therefore His purpose in the world can become our purpose as well.

> *'but whoever drinks of the water that I shall give him will never thirst; the water that I shall give him will become in him a spring of water welling up to eternal life.'*
>
> (John 4:14)

As we drink of the water that Christ gives us, His life wells up in us, so that we may become full of His life within us. We become in Him a spring of water welling up to eternal life enabling us to share His word with others, or pray for others, even with signs and healings and miracles as Jesus also did on this earth. Simply drinking daily in His presence from His living waters, His Holy Spirit can enable us to walk on this earth in a new dimension in **His life**, and **His life** will radiate through our lives wherever we go.

> *'In Him was **life**, and the **life** was the light of men. The light shines in the darkness, and darkness has not overcome it.'*
>
> (John 1:4–5)

Life also means light, for Christ is **life** and **light**. Death and the devil live in darkness and darkness cannot understand, fathom, grasp, comprehend, overcome or come near the light. Where the light shines darkness disappears even as the sunrise of a new day conquers all darkness bringing the dark world back into the light of day. When we spend time in worship, the Lord fills our body with His light which brings healing, refreshment and redemption into our dark world, through us. Through us He can shine His light that shows the way and brings truth and hope to all men.

> *'For the gate is narrow and the way is hard, that leads to life, and those who find it are few.'*   (Matthew 7:14)

How much more then do we need to warn man, for those who do not allow the Lord into their lives cannot partake of the life that He is willing to give.

> *'The fear of the LORD is a fountain of life,*
> *that one may avoid the snares of death.'*
>   (Proverbs 14:27)

Fear and reverence of the Lord means that we can submit our lives into His care. He can give us the fountain of life and protect us from the snares of death.

> *'In the path of righteousness is **life**,*
> *but the way of error leads to death.'*   (Proverbs 12:28)

Only Jesus is the true path to righteousness.
    Proverbs 3:22 says of **wisdom** and discretion:

> *'and they will be life for your soul*
> *and adornment for your neck.*

Wisdom means life for your soul. In Jesus we find God and come to know Him and in knowing God we find and have life:

> *'For with thee is the fountain of **life**;*
> *in thy light do we see light.'* (Psalm 36:9)

> *'Thou dost show me the path of **life**;*
> *in thy presence there is fullness of joy,*
> *in thy right hand are pleasures for evermore.'*
>
> (Psalm 16:11)

Only by coming into the presence of God can He show you His beautiful presence, can He fill you with His incredible joy. No pleasure on this earth can compare with it. All the peace, all the joy, all the excitement or entertainment that the world can give is momentary, temporary, but the love, joy and peace of the Lord are constant. They stay with you through life and the closer we keep to Him, the more we realise the joy of His touch upon our lives. It is real, it is deep and it is beautiful.

> *'to bring back his soul from the Pit,*
> *that he may see **the light of life**.'* (Job 33:30)

Christ brings up the soul from the pit by going down into the pit after it, and may well use His people to do this, which will enable man to turn from the darkness of sin and death to see the light of life in Jesus our Saviour instead.

> *'The spirit of God has made me,*
> *and the breath of the Almighty gives me **life**.'*
>
> (Job 33:4)

The Holy Spirit of God is also the breath of God. The

translation from Greek means 'spirit and breath'. Therefore
the breath of God gives life.

> *'Loving the* LORD *your God, obeying his voice, and cleaving to*
> *him; for that means* **life to you** *and length of days, that you*
> *may dwell in the land which the* LORD *swore to your fathers,*
> *to Abraham, to Isaac, and to Jacob, to give them.'*
> (Deuteronomy 30:20)

When we love the Lord we will obey Him. We will cleave to
Him for He means everything to us. He is our life, He is
everything we ever need to walk this life on earth and to do
the work that He has called us to do. This we will do with joy,
for we will want to be pleasing to Him.

> *'See, I have set before you this day life and good, death and*
> *evil.'*   (Deuteronomy 30:15)

He has loved us so much that He has given us free choice: **life**
and goodness in Him, or death and evil without Him. It is
the Lord who makes the rules. It is so much better to come to
Him and live.

> *'And out of the ground the* LORD *God made to grow every tree*
> *that is pleasant to the sight and good for food, the tree of* **life**
> *also in the midst of the garden, and the tree of the knowledge*
> *of good and evil.'*   (Genesis 2:9)

God always allows us to eat from the tree of life because that
life comes ever new from Him. But Adam and Eve ate from
the forbidden tree, the tree of the knowledge of good and
evil, hence our lives on this earth of good and evil.

It is interesting that the Lord showed me these scriptures
in the opposite direction than I would normally study them.
We began in Revelation starting with the tree of life and

ended in Genesis with the tree of life. Could the Lord be saying to us, that our lives on this earth, fighting against evil and what Jesus has done for us on the cross, is bringing us once again back to the place Adam and Eve had in God, before the fall? That this earth, with all its evil within, may be used by God to separate those who belong to Him from those who do not belong to Him? To use the evil in this world to help form a strong character within us? For if we resist evil here on earth, then definitely we will not turn from God in heaven.

True strength is not power or might, but to know what is right and to stand for the truth, no matter how high the cost is. This earth with all its difficulties can also help to refine us and make us become more Christ-like.

Our lives upon this earth, as we love and serve our Lord against any opposition that may try and come our way to prevent us, can actually bring us back to the original plan that God created us for, to have fellowship with Him and to live a full **life** with Him for all eternity.

I felt the Lord saying to me, 'I am **life** indeed, and you are finding it in me. **I am life, I am love, I am vitality, I am peace, I am joy, I am the living water**. Tell the world that **I AM** has come. The more you receive from Me, the more your life shall become My life. So shall your life be quickened, so shall your life shine forth My life and your life shall release My life in power, through your life, in the healing and setting free of My people.'

God does not just have love, joy, peace, etc. He actually **is** love, joy, peace, etc. These qualities are part of His character defined by Him, exhibited by Him and characterised by Him. For instance we may posses strength, but only God **is** strength. What we would possess some of, the Lord **is** that and always has been.

God said to Moses, '*I AM WHO I AM*' (Exodus 3:14). Jesus also said in John 8:58, '*Truly, truly, I say to you, before Abraham was, I am.'*. In John 11:25 Jesus said to Martha, *'I am the resurrection and the life'*, and to the disciples in John 6:35, *'I am the bread of life'*. Neither God nor Jesus ever said, 'I was', or 'I will be', they said, **'I am'** and Revelation 22:13 says, *'I am the Alpha and the Omega, the first and the last, the beginning and the end.'*

He who was and is and will be, **is now**, for God and Jesus live outside time so **all** that **Jesus is, is with us now** and for all eternity.

We began with the tree of life and end with the tree of life, demonstrating the pattern of constant renewal by God, in God, and through God. By His one everlasting sacrifice offered upon the cross, we have His continual life working through our lives. **He is now** our love, joy, peace, renewal, strength, healing, deliverance, forgiveness, life. **He is** everything we ever need, at the moment of every need. **He is** our victory, accomplished 2,000 years ago on the cross. By His stripes we are healed. By His death on the cross we are forgiven. By His resurrection we receive our gift of eternal life. We can have His victory now, for He won us our victory over Satan 2,000 years ago. All we have to do is receive it.

His unlimited gift of what He did on the cross spans past, present and future in the power of forgiveness and everlasting new life in Christ.

Through forgiveness of sin man can rise into the Lord's unlimited grace, love and peace, beautiful beyond description. Man does not have to wait for death. Prayer can take us there. Whether crying with joy at the feet of Him who touched and walked this earth for us or dancing before Him in the joy of His love, we can experience a touch of His glorious splendour. His touch upon our lives transforms us and makes us whole.

Jesus shed His blood upon the cross for our forgiveness of sin and for eternal life. Jesus gave His body upon the cross for the physical healing of our bodies. He therefore died to free the whole man both spiritually and physically. Should we then not receive Him anew each day? Allow His Holy Spirit to transform our lives, let all negative things to go – sin, sickness, hurts, unforgiveness, demons, curses, problems etc. – and receive from Him instead all the positive things such as love, joy, peace, health, freedom, prosperity and **life in Him**.

So His Holy Spirit brings eternal life into our mortal bodies and transforms us into His life. All negative things of death within us go and all positive things within us become our life. Jesus said, *'I came that they may have life, and have it abundantly'* (John 10:10).

We can have life abundantly, and more abundantly as we begin to see things from a higher perspective – something higher and greater than the world we see around us. Is it the glorious victory of Jesus over all the forces of evil and darkness? Is it a moving into the glorious victory of Jesus over sickness and hurt and even death? Is it seeing the victory of Jesus over the hurts of this world almost visibly? Abundant life is like the expanse of His beauty and strength and majesty, clean and open and pure, His greatness, His love and compassion, bringing life and healing and hope to the people on this earth. I see abundant life as immense victory, the opening of the heavens, immense joy, immense love, the immense greatness of our Lord Jesus shining forth brilliant light and fullness of life.

Is it possible to move into this realm, to live in this realm in Him? To see the miraculous? To live in constant victory in Him over all the forces of evil? To see sickness and evil crumble under your feet, as you bring the victory of Jesus to the peoples? 'Lord, are You showing me this?' I asked.

The Lord replied, 'Why do you doubt? See My hands and My feet, put your hand to My side.'

I responded, 'My Lord, my God, resurrected one, victorious over all life and death.'

I felt the Lord saying, 'Do you now comprehend, My child, the victory in Me that I call you to?'

I felt as small as an ant and replied, 'Yes, I will walk in it, with You Lord, only with You.'

He replied, 'Place your hand in mine. Never let go of it, for this path we shall walk together. For this path can only be walked with Me.'

'Lord,' I asked, 'please let me never let go of Your hand, for I feel I am walking on the water with You. Without You I would surely sink.'

'Here,' He replied, 'take My hand, for I shall never let go of My child. Keep close to Me and we shall walk together.'

To live with the expanse of heaven in the confines of this earth is how Jesus lived! He spent hours in prayer with the Father where He received of the unlimited supernatural power of heaven. This is what enabled Jesus to walk on water, calm the storm, cast out demons, heal the sick and raise the dead, and He tells us to do the same. We are limited in every way, but the Lord is unlimited by time, space, thought and capability. Time with Him in prayer lifts you out of the limits of your own life into His. Here His supernatural ability transcends your own, causing you to walk in a higher dimension and authority.

Chapter 13

Worship in Spirit and Truth

Worship is the highest form of service we can give the Lord, for worship is to Him and to worship Him is what we are created for – to bring Him joy, to be in relationship with Him.

Who are we to be called to such a joy of knowing Him, to such a destiny as dwelling in His glorious presence? As for me, I have discovered that the more I come to know Him, the lower I need to bow to His greatness, for the bigger I see Him, the more I am humbled. The day I saw the Lord answer His people's prayer for rain within the hour, above all the healings He did that day, made me cry with gratitude for the great love and compassion that He showed to His people. Moses must have felt a similar way, as the Lord led the children of Israel through the Red Sea and supplied manna daily for them in the wilderness. Oh, the awesomeness and greatness of our living God! I felt at the time that I barely knew Him, for He showed Himself to us in such a way that day greater than I could ever have imagined. If we read of Paul's life we see that he, too, discovered the same thing. At his conversion he saw himself as special, as some of us do when God first calls us.

> *'And from those who were reputed to be something (what they were makes no difference to me; God shows no partiality) – those, I say, who were of repute added nothing to me.'*
>
> (Galatians 2:6)

Later Paul thinks differently:

> *'For I am the least of the apostles, unfit to be called an apostle, because I persecuted the church of God.'*
>
> (1 Corinthians 15:9)

As he grows further in the Lord he has this to say in Ephesians 3:8

> *'To me, though I am the very least of all the saints, this grace was given, to preach to the Gentiles the unsearchable riches of Christ.'*

Then in 1 Timothy 1:15

> *'The saying is sure and worthy and full of acceptance, that Christ Jesus came into the world to save sinners. And I am the foremost of sinners.'*

What has happened here? Paul has not come lower; only the opinion he has of himself compared to the greatness of the Lord which has been revealed to him. He has in fact grown far closer to the Lord, and grown more Christ-like, so next to the majesty and splendour of his God he had to bow lower.

So it is only through what Jesus alone has done for us that we have through Him this priceless privilege of coming to know God, the King of kings, and to dwell in His presence. Compared to His greatness we are very very small indeed and the bigger we see Him the smaller we see ourselves.

So now, who is this great God whom we worship? Let's see who John says He is in Revelation 1:4–8:

> *'John to the seven churches that are in Asia:*
>
> *Grace to you and peace from **him who is and who was and who is to come**, and from the seven spirits who are before his throne, and from **Jesus Christ** the faithful witness, the first-born of the dead, and the ruler of kings on earth. To him who loves us and has freed us from our sins by his blood and made us a kingdom, priests to his God and Father, to him be glory and dominion forever and ever. Amen. Behold, he is coming with the clouds, and every eye will see him, every one who pierced him; and all the tribes of the earth will wail on account of him. Even so. Amen.*
>
> *"I am the Alpha and the Omega," says the Lord God, **who is and who was and who is to come, the Almighty**.'*

Now let's see how the living creatures see God:

> *'And the four living creatures, each of them with six wings, are full of eyes all round and within, and day and night they never cease to sing,*
> *"**Holy, holy, holy**, is the **Lord God Almighty**,*
> *who was and is and is to come!"'* (Revelation 4:8)

Let's now see how the elders see God:

> *'And the twenty-four elders who sit on their thrones before God fell on their faces and worshipped God, saying,*
> *"We give thanks to thee, **Lord God Almighty, who art and who wast**,*
> *that thou hast taken thy great power and begun to reign."'* (Revelation 11:16–17)

Now the angels, during the pouring out of the wrath of

God upon the people who disobeyed God at the end of the age:

> *'The third angel poured his bowl into the rivers and the fountains of water, and they became blood. And I heard the angel of water say,*
> > *"Just art thou in these thy judgements, thou **who art and wast, O Holy One."**'*   (Revelation 16:4–5)

The plagues at the end of the age are similar to those God poured out on Egypt to release His chosen people, the Jews. God is Almighty, the God of Abraham, Isaac and Jacob, the God of Moses, the God of His chosen nation, the Jews, the God of every believer who has ever walked on this earth, the God of all eternity, of all the heavens and earth. **He** and only **He is**.

Yet this great God calls to feeble mankind like us and says in Jeremiah 33:3:

> *'Call to me and I will answer you, and will tell you great and hidden things which you have not known.'*

So how do we call upon this great God **who was and is and is to come**?

> *'Honour and majesty are before him;*
> > *strength and joy are in his place.*
> *Ascribe to the* LORD, *O families of the peoples,*
> > *ascribe to the* LORD *glory and strength!*
> *Ascribe to the* LORD *the glory due his name;*
> > *bring an offering, and come before him!*
> *Worship the* LORD *in holy array.'*
>
> (1 Chronicles 16:27–29)

What offering can we bring Him?

'*For thou hast no delight in sacrifice;*
  were I to give a burnt offering, thou wouldst not be
    pleased.
The sacrifice acceptable to God is a broken spirit;
  a broken and contrite heart, O God, thou wilt not
    despise.'   (Psalm 51:16–17)

'*To do righteousness and justice*
  is more acceptable to the Lord *than sacrifice.'*
                                            (Proverbs 21:3)

' *"and to love him with all the heart, and with all the*
understanding, and with all the strength, and to love one's
neighbour as oneself, is much more than all whole burnt
offerings and sacrifices." And when Jesus saw that he
answered wisely, he said to him, "You are not far from the
kingdom of God."'   (Mark 12:33–34)

We need to worship God with the offering of ourselves to
Him, of our very lives to Him, for He alone is worthy.
Worship to God is not only what we pour out of ourselves
to His feet upon His throne, but the very lives we live out for
others upon this earth. It's all that we are, all that we ever
hope to be, given up for Him, now and forever. That is the
highest form of sacrifice we can give Him, the greatest
offering we are capable of giving God, ourselves, and our
lives. Our only opportunity to give Him anything is here on
this earth, in loving Him and others as ourselves.

'*Ascribe to the* Lord, *O heavenly beings,*
  ascribe to the Lord *glory and strength.*
Ascribe to the Lord *the glory of his name;*
  worship the Lord *in holy array.*
The voice of the Lord *is upon the waters;*
  the God of glory thunders,
  the Lord, *upon many waters.*

The voice of the Lord is powerful,
  the voice of the LORD is full of majesty.'   (Psalm 29:1–4)

Here all the heavenly beings worship Him and as we read again in Hebrews that all God's angels worship Him:

'*And again, when he brings the first-born into the world, he says,*
  "Let all God's angels worship him."
Of the angels he says,
  "Who makes his angels winds,
  and his servants flames of fire."
But of the Son he says,
  "Thy throne, O God, is for ever and ever,
  the righteous sceptre is the sceptre of thy kingdom."'

(Hebrews 1:6–8)

We are able in worship to join the angels of heaven and every living creature in heaven, to worship Him, who is King of kings and Lord of lords:

'*O come, let us worship and bow down,*
  let us kneel before the LORD, our Maker!
For he is our God,
  and we are the people of his pasture,
  and the sheep of his hand.'   (Psalm 95:6–7)

'*Worship the LORD in holy array;*
  tremble before him, all the earth!'   (Psalm 96:9)

'*Let us go to his dwelling place;*
  let us worship at his footstool!'   (Psalm 132:7)

Yes, let us worship at His footstool, let us rise up in worship until His presence surrounds us and fills us with His incredible joy, His wonderful love, His everlasting peace.

Let us worship in the way Jesus called us to worship Him in
John 4:23–24:

> *'But the hour is coming, and now is, when the true worship-*
> *pers will worship the Father in spirit and truth, for such the*
> *Father seeks to worship him. God is spirit, and those who*
> *worship him, must worship in spirit and truth.'*

When we respond to this scripture, a deeper level awaits,
that of a heart-to-heart connection in Him, to become one in
Him, a giving yourself to Him and receiving His love which
transcends your mind, emotions, heart and body, seeping
into every part, until in Him you feel absorbed.

We are so indebted, so helpless, next to what He has done
for us, given to us, through salvation and love. We have
nothing to give God other than our heart and He receives it
as precious, and then gives to you a touch of His heart,
holding them together to become as one heart in Him.

A belonging, a union in Him. Allow Him to anoint your
heart with His, to rub some of His love and character into
yours. For the Lord said to me, 'For this is the life I have
called you to. To become one with Me, I in you and you in
Me, to fill you with My love, to anoint you with My holy oil,
that you may walk forth in the world as a radiant witness for
Me. So go forth in joy, My child, for I am surely with you.'

As you respond to Him, and begin to come closer and
closer to Him in worship, He will change you, fill you with
His love and call you to new life in Him, for this is the life He
has called us to.

Prayer is the only unlimited treasure on this earth. All
other things are limited. Only prayer can take one into the
unlimited realms of the heavenlies, into the very presence of
God. Here Jesus is unlimited in beauty, with unlimited love
that is deeper than the deepest ocean, higher than the
highest heavens and wider than the widest horizons. His

joy and peace are likewise. Even His patience and kindness extend beyond all limits.

Available to each one of us is unlimited access into such beauty in Him; not visible but heartfelt, relational, silent heart connection with indescribable joy and peace and beauty. This is meant for us, kept for us, reachable, attainable, but only through Jesus. For this is all about Him, a giving and receiving, no words, just heartfelt connection, a blending, a melting, a cleansing, a filling of calm beauty and love, like warm oil seeping into every crevice of your being.

There is no better place to be than alone with the Lord. He touches your heart with such gentleness, a contact with Him that is so so precious. This access into Him is unlimited. It involves yielding to the changes He effects in your life and flowing with Him who created all things.

Come to Him and He will lead you into all truth. Churches and conferences can teach, books can educate and encourage, but nothing can compare with coming to the Master Himself, our Lord. Nothing can replace Him. Nothing can touch or compare to coming into His presence. Nothing but knowing the reality of the Lord yourself. Only He can reach your heart.

Chapter 14

To Rejoice in Him

We can rise up into the thermals of His presence and experience silent glory, lifting higher, weightless on wings of worship, connecting with Him in the beauty of His radiance, His calm, His peace.

Like a garment, His presence covers your being. In Him you are surrendered to do His will. His radiance electrifies your being into life, health, vision and boldness – His life transcending your own, changing, transforming, perfecting, beautifying, new life – it's supernatural.

You walk this new life in Him, His presence radiating within, giving courage, conviction, faith in Him for His works, watching Jesus do His work. **He is**, **He does**, **He changes things, He is, everlastingly is**.

> '*I will greatly rejoice in the LORD,*
> *my soul shall exult in my God;*
> *for he has clothed me with the garments of salvation,*
> *he has covered me with the robe of righteousness,*
> *as a bridegroom decks himself with a garland,*
> *and as a bride adorns herself with her jewels.'*

(Isaiah 61:10)

How can this be? Only by coming to Jesus, receiving His

forgiveness and new life, can free us to become in Him what He originally created us to become.

> *'Blessed be the God and Father of our Lord Jesus Christ! By his great mercy we have been born anew to a living hope through the resurrection of Jesus Christ from the dead, and to an inheritance which is imperishable, undefiled, and unfading, kept in heaven for you, who by God's power are guarded through faith for a salvation ready to be revealed in the last time. In this you rejoice, though now for a little while you may have to suffer various trials, so that the genuineness of your faith, more precious than gold which though perishable is tested by fire, may redound to praise and glory and honour at the revelation of **Jesus Christ**. Without having seen him you love him; though you do not now see him you believe in him and rejoice with unutterable and exalted joy. As the outcome of your faith you obtain the salvation of your souls.'*
>
> (1 Peter 1:3–9)

Also in Romans we read:

> *'For if while we were enemies we were reconciled to God by the death of his Son, much more, now that we are reconciled, shall we be saved by his life. Not only so, but we also rejoice in God through our Lord Jesus Christ, through whom we have now received our reconciliation.'*
>
> (Romans 5:10–11)

When we receive what Jesus has done for us and live this life out for Him, so God will rejoice over us.

> *'For as a young man marries a virgin,*
>   *so shall your sons marry you,*
> *and as the bridegroom rejoices over the bride,*
>   *so shall your God rejoice over you.'*   (Isaiah 62:5)

Is this not the highest rejoicing we can ever know, God and man rejoicing over each other, rejoicing out of pure love? He has done such great and mighty works for us.

> *'As he was drawing near, at the descent of the Mount of Olives, the whole multitude of the disciples began to rejoice and praise God with a loud voice for all the mighty works that they had seen.'* (Luke 19:37)

Let us rejoice in Him, let us praise His name.

> *'This is the day which the LORD has made;*
> *let us rejoice and be glad in it.'* (Psalm 118:24)

> *'Then my soul shall rejoice in the LORD,*
> *exulting in his deliverance.'* (Psalm 35:9)

> *'But let all who take refuge in thee rejoice,*
> *let them ever sing for joy;*
> *and do thou defend them,*
> *that those who love thy name may exult in thee.*
> *For thou dost bless the righteous, O LORD,*
> *thou dost cover him with favour as with a shield.'*
> (Psalm 5:11–12)

These are wonderful, wonderful promises to rejoice over. Nothing on this earth can compare with the glorious exalted joy that we find in Jesus through what He has done for us.

It is His presence within that becomes the source of our life and being. It is the heart connection we find in Him. We can get so close into the presence of God that His presence becomes almost thick on us, that it stays with us during the whole day. Maybe seeking this presence may take hours, but it is so worth it. Then the Lord may speak to you as He did to me:

'Yes, My child, seek My presence continually for truly this is the essence of life, for surely this is the essence of your faith. This is where your life can become a sweet aroma pleasing in My sight. This is where your life and ministry takes on a new dimension in Me. This is when My Holy Spirit can operate through your life. This is when you shall see Me move through you in ways that will make you marvel, for it shall be I, your Holy God, that shall do it.'

He then showed me a scripture that made me have to read what He showed me a second time at a deeper level.

> *'Sing to him, sing praises to him,*
> *   tell of all his wonderful works!*
> *Glory in his holy name;*
> *   let the hearts of those who seek the LORD rejoice!*
> *Seek the LORD and his strength,*
> *   seek his presence continually!'*   (1 Chronicles 16:9–11)

To live in the presence of God continually is to seek Him continually, not just the time set aside for Him, but through-out the day, during the daily chores and activities. This will help us to dwell in Jesus moment by moment. This will cause us to test each action before we do it, to hopefully stay away from sin.

This constant living for Him is a powerful new dimension, to be fully surrendered to Him. I know I need the Lord every second of my life, that His will may be done in and through my life, to be clothed in His presence continually. As Isaiah 61:10 says: *'he has clothed me with the garments of salvation.'* Is this continual clothing of His presence, along with the spiritual armour of Ephesians 6:13–18, the garment of salvation?

> *'Therefore take the whole armour of God, that you may be able to withstand in the evil day, and having done all, to*

stand. Stand therefore, having girded your loins with truth, and having put on the breastplate of righteousness, and having shod your feet with the equipment of the gospel of peace; besides all these, taking the shield of faith, with which you can quench all the flaming darts of the evil one. And take the helmet of salvation, and the sword of the Spirit, which is the word of God. Pray at all times in the Spirit, with all prayer and supplication. To that end keep alert with all persever- ance, making supplication for all the saints.'

If we put on then the armour of God complete with the garment of salvation that gives us the covering or garment of His glorious presence and the robe of righteousness, what else can we ever need to live this glorious life in Him, to become pleasing in His sight and to do His will on earth while we are still alive? This is the way of rejoicing, for all that we have to give up, in order to follow Him, is as rubbish, compared to the riches of our life and inheritance in Him.

Whether we worship Him in silence or out loud, in whispers or in singing, in tears or in joy, in groans or in dancing, all is worship. Whether you worship in prayer or intercession for others, in waiting on Him, or in service toward others in kindness or witnessing, all is worship unto God. All is valued in the same way. Sometimes putting your own words or prayers to music that you hear, or praying Scripture is of value, until your whole life becomes a song of worship into His ear, a sweet aroma of incense that joins with all the prayers of all the saints throughout history, in anticipation of a very historic half hour which is to come:

'When the Lamb opened the seventh seal, there was silence in heaven for about half an hour. Then I saw the seven angels who stand before God, and seven trumpets were given to them. And another angel came and stood at the altar with a golden censer; and he was given much incense to mingle with

*the prayers of all the saints upon the golden altar before the
throne; and the smoke of the incense rose with the prayers of
the saints from the hand of the angel before God.'*

(Revelation 8:1–4)

This scripture can be life-changing in itself, knowing that
God values our prayers so much as to silence heaven for half
an hour. It is awesome. Please know you are special to Jesus. If
you have not responded yet, do pray the prayer of salvation,
or to receive the Holy Spirit, or the prayer of dedication
to serve Him. I challenge you not to wait, for Jesus is a 'now'
God and now is the time to respond for later may be too
late.

All who have responded in some way, or have been
challenged to go deeper with the Lord shall rejoice with all
the saints:

'Rejoice in the LORD, O you righteous!
  Praise befits the upright.
Praise the LORD with the lyre,
  make melody to him with the harp of ten strings!
Sing to him a new song,
  play skilfully on the strings, with loud shouts.'

(Psalm 33:1–3)

'Rejoice in the Lord always; again I will say, Rejoice.'

(Philippians 4:4)

To rejoice in Him, to know Him, is the most incredible
exulted joy one can ever know, to feel His joy bubble up
within, connected to Him with such strong cords of love that
nothing can separate. There is no greater joy, there is no
greater truth. Jesus is the way, the truth, the life, such
abundant life, the greatest abundance of love, joy and peace.
Only in Jesus can we find it, only in Jesus can we live it, this

joyful love connection with the King of kings and Lord of lords. This we can live for.

There was I time when I asked, 'How can I spend more time with God? How can I ever keep it up?' But once I did try the Lord gave me the grace to keep it up and it has become my greatest joy.

To end this book – which I don't want to do, for it has been such a privilege and joy to write – let's use this as a beginning with the Lord, a foundation to build on in prayer, in coming to know our wonderful Lord so much more.

> *'For this reason I bow my knees before the Father, from whom every family in heaven and on earth is named, that according to the riches of his glory he may grant you to be strengthened with might through his Spirit in the inner man, and that Christ may dwell in your hearts through faith; that you, being rooted and grounded in love, may have power to comprehend with all the saints what is the breadth and length and height and depth, and to know the love of Christ which surpasses knowledge, that you may be filled with all the fullness of God.'*   (Ephesians 3:14–19)

The more we come to know our God, the greater our joy.

A prayer for salvation or recommitment

Dear Lord Jesus, I come to You as I am. Please forgive me, when I have sinned in thought, in word, in deed, in things left undone, and please come into my life as my Lord and Saviour. Thank You, Lord. Amen.

A prayer for baptism in the Holy Spirit

Please baptise me in Your Holy Spirit that I can be more effective for You. Thank You, Lord. Amen.

Now just receive Him. He will also enable you to pray more effectively daily, and read your Bible with more understanding. Join a church or Christian fellowship and tell someone of your new commitment to the Lord.

If you should require further prayer, you are welcome to contact me (see page 127 for details).

May God bless you, may His hand be upon your life as you live out your Christian life day by day, allowing the Lord to guide you and help you live it out. May He strengthen you and fill you with His perfect love, joy, and peace. Amen.

A thought on serving the Lord effectively

It's not how many hours we spend in prayer
but the degree that we know Him.

It's not how much we can do for the Lord
but the amount of love that we serve Him with.

It's not the size of the anointing we have
but the degree we die to self to release Him.

It's not what **we** can do for the Lord
but what **He** can do through us.

The Standlake Equestrian Centre and Adventure Ranch is an interdenominational riding school, residential ranch and outreach centre, devoted to encouraging people in the Lord and to the spreading of the gospel in any way possible.

The new adventure ranch opened in the Summer of 2003. It has accommodation facilities for forty people.

People can also come and stay in woodland chalets overlooking natural reed beds.

Ministry for healing and wholeness is available along with horse riding, woodland walks, boating and relaxation.

For more information or for ordering books write to:

Suzanne Pillans
Standlake Equestrian Centre and Adventure Ranch
Downs Road
Standlake
Witney
Oxfordshire OX29 7UH

Tel: 01865 300099
Email: (wpillans@aol.com)